LAMDA
ACTING ANTHOLOGY

Volume 3

The LAMDA *Acting Anthology (Volume 3)*

First published in 2014 by the London Academy of Music and Dramatic Art
155 Talgarth Road, London W14 9DA, United Kingdom
Tel: +44 (0)844 847 0520 / Fax: +44 (0)844 847 0521
www.lamda.org.uk

A catalogue record for this book is available from the British Library.

Printed by: Consider This UK
Cover image: Thinkstock
Concept design and layout: Cambridge Design Consultants

ISBN: 9780955768774

The LAMDA *Acting Anthology (Volume 3)* is a collection of solo and duologue scenes and is a required publication for learners taking LAMDA *Graded Examinations in Performance: Acting* from Grade 1 to Grade 5.

You may notice that in the case of certain acting scenes, spelling of some words may vary from piece to piece, representing either standard British or American spelling. This is because we have maintained the spelling found in the original source material.

Contents

Contents *continued*

Level 1 Acting: Grade 3 Duologue

Level 2 Acting: Grade 4 Solo

Level 2 Acting: Grade 4 Duologue

Level 2 Acting: Grade 5 Solo

Level 2 Acting: Grade 5 Duologue

Introduction

It gives me great pleasure as a Vice-President of the London Academy of Music and Dramatic Art to have been invited to write the introduction for this LAMDA *Acting Anthology*.

Within these covers can be found a treasure trove of so many varying speeches and themes, every one of which has been very carefully chosen and designed in order to challenge and, perhaps most of all, to inspire and excite. The scenes and speeches range from Charles Dickens' *The Haunting of Ebenezer Scrooge* to Clifford Jury's *Acting Class*, from Shaun McKenna's *Below Stairs* to George Bernard Shaw's *Androcles and the Lion*, and even a piece from Dorothy in *The Wizard of Oz*. Of course, there are also some passages by William Shakespeare.

Anyone who is approaching the challenging and perhaps daunting task of preparing an examination passage will be able to choose from a wealth of literary material within this anthology, any and all of which will be so very beneficial.

The LAMDA exams are very well known worldwide, and in taking the exam the performer is given the rare opportunity of opening windows upon a huge array of styles that will allow natural talent to be seen or displayed.

I had a great deal of pleasure in reading through the anthology myself and, above all, I do hope most sincerely that in the reading, choosing, preparing and performing of these carefully chosen extracts, there will be a huge sense of enjoyment that will surpass the sometimes daunting experience of taking an examination.

I am convinced that among these very varying excellent speeches and scenes there will be something for everyone who wishes to display their full artistic performing talents.

David Suchet (CBE)

Actor and Vice-President of LAMDA

Thanks

LAMDA would like to thank all of the authors, publishers and agents who made the development of this anthology possible. Special thanks are also due to Clarissa Aykroyd, Jacque Emery, Vivien Heilbron, Linda Macrow, Sandra McDowell, Pauline Stevens and Julia Watson.

Level 1 Acting

Grade 1 Solo

Titles in Level 1 Acting: Grade 1 Solo

Alice In Wonderland

ALICE has fallen down the rabbit hole and finds herself in a world populated by talking animals and strange people, full of riddles and mysteries. In this scene, she tries to join a mad tea party.

ALICE: *(Entering a clearing in the woods)* This must be where the Hatter lives – there is a table under a tree outside the house – Oh look – that poor Dormouse – the Hare and the Hatter are using it as a cushion – resting their elbows on it and talking over its head! Very uncomfortable for the Dormouse – only as it's asleep I suppose it doesn't mind. I think I'll go and join them. *(She attempts to sit down and join them, and they try to send her away)* No room! There's plenty of room *(pointing to the empty table and sitting down)*. I'm sorry if you think I sat down without being invited – but I didn't know it was *your* table! I actually think you are very rude – telling me to cut my hair too. You should learn not to make personal remarks! *(Smiling)* I'm glad you want to play games now. Riddles are fun. Perhaps the Dormouse will wake up and join in! *(Looking at it)* Well, perhaps not. What's the first one then? "Why is a raven like a writing-desk?" *(Thinks)* I believe I can guess that. I always say what I mean – at least I mean what I say. That's the same thing you know. *(Thinking)* I haven't guessed the riddle yet. What's the answer? You don't know either. Well. I think you might do something better with the time than waste it asking riddles with no answers! Stories! Now that's more interesting. *(Pausing and watching them pinch the Dormouse on both sides at once)* You'll hurt him! Now I shall really enjoy listening to his story but you'd better be quick or he'll be asleep again before it's done! *(To the Hatter)* How dare you tell me not to talk. I'm going! *(Getting up)* And stop trying to put the Dormouse into the teapot. *(Walking off into the wood)*

by Lewis Carroll, adapted by LAMDA

The Necklace of Fingers

This scene is based on an ancient story from India. ANGULIMALA is a terrifying robber who cuts off his victims' fingers and hangs them on a necklace. He is famous for his terrible deeds, and most people stay far away from him. Today, though, another unsuspecting victim is wandering down Angulimala's road.

ANGULIMALA:

(Leaping on to the acting space, he glowers at the audience)

Ha! Ha! I am Angulimala, a Brigand, and I love causing fear and trouble. In the Kingdom of Kosala, I am known and feared by everyone. I am worse than any catastrophe… like a flood or a plague or a war. It's because I have made a vow to kill one thousand people. To keep count, I cut off a finger of each victim and make it into a necklace. See.

(Hanging around his neck is a necklace of fingers which he lovingly shows to the audience)

They are lovely. Are they not? Delightful… and I have only a few more fingers to collect.

(He goes closer to the audience and makes threatening eye focus where possible)

I have to work hard and long hours at being nasty and cruel; and I'll not stop until I have a complete necklace. Ha! Ha! It's great fun!

Villages have become empty because of me. People have gone to live in the safety of cities because of me… People will not go out at night because of me…

Did you know, even the King's men have tried to catch me?... but I can run faster than the fastest horse; and I'm so strong.

(He shows his muscles to the audience)

Once the King sent out forty men on horseback to get me; but I have brains as well, and I led them a merry dance. By the time they had gone around and around… *(He spins around and around)* they were so dizzy I just knocked them, one by one, off their horses, killed them, and collected their fingers.

Forty. Yes, forty of them. All in one day. That was a good day that was!

(He looks to his left, away from the acting space)

Ah! Another traveller, and all on his own, wandering down my road. *(Rubbing his hands together)* He will pass right by my lair. (*(Aside)* He obviously has not heard of me.) I must hurry and climb into my hiding place, so that I am ready to pounce on him and get another finger for my necklace. *(He moves down stage right, and crouches down as if in his lair and waits. The traveller draws closer. He then leaps out, holds his upstage hand up and shouts out menacingly)* Stop!

by Jill O'Hare

Molly

MOLLY has to play the piano because her parents want her to, but she is not happy about it. Here she describes why piano lessons are no fun at all.

MOLLY: I have to take these stupid piano lessons every Wednesday after school. From old Mrs Campbell. She's like this big tall lady who lives over on Euclid Avenue. She has a great big grand piano in her living room where she teaches a whole bunch of kids. Her house is always freezing cold in the winter. (*She shivers*) Mrs Campbell sits next to me on the piano bench and yells at me when I make a mistake. I hate piano lessons and I tell my mom I do but she doesn't listen. Nobody listens to kids.

I'm in the beginners' book. It's supposed to be real easy, but it isn't. It's real hard. The hardest part for me is trying to keep the right time. I can't. Even though Mrs Campbell counts out loud. *(She impersonates Mrs Campbell counting aloud)* "One-two-three-four, one-two-three-four." So far, after almost a year, all I can play are these dumb little pieces. Mostly only with my right hand. My left hand doesn't work right. *(She makes awkward, piano playing movements with her left hand)*

I have to practice every day, too. While other kids are out playing, I have to stay in and do my piano lesson. I keep telling Mom how much I hate it but she says I have talent. Know what? Having talent isn't any fun.

by Ruth Mae Roddy

The Wizard of Oz

DOROTHY and her little dog Toto live on a farm in Kansas with her Auntie Em and Uncle Henry. The nasty Miss Gulch, who dislikes Toto, is her worst enemy. One day, a terrible cyclone strikes, whirling the house, Dorothy and Toto away to the Land of Oz.

DOROTHY: Auntie Em! Auntie Em! Oh dear Toto – the cyclone is coming closer. What shall we do? We haven't time to get down to the storm shelter. Ouch! That hurt! *(Debris begins to fly around her)* There goes the window! There's swirling dust everywhere! The house is spinning up through dust. Look Toto! Watch out! We're not on the ground any more, Toto! There's the chicken coop! And an old lady sitting in a rocking chair. Knitting! She's flying through the sky! And look – there's a cow! A cow – just floating past! And a rowing boat. *(DOROTHY tries to stand up – away from the bed – but ducks to avoid a floating tree)* Whoops! That was a tree! *And* it nearly hit me! We must be up inside the cyclone. *(She sits on the edge of the bed, watching the world pass by her)* There's Miss Gulch, Toto – on her bicycle. Quick Toto – hide! She mustn't see you! She hasn't forgiven you for chasing her nasty old cat! I hate her! Oh Toto – look – the bicycle – it's changed into a broomstick! And her clothes – she's wearing a flying robe – and a pointed hat! *(DOROTHY lies face down on the bed, covering her eyes)* Has she gone Toto? I'm scared. Everything is spinning round us. *(Screaming)* Round… and round… the house is turning – spinning – twirling – the cyclone is whirling! Louder… and louder… Help! We're coming down! We're falling through the air. We're going to crash. *(They land with a thud. DOROTHY waits a moment. She lets go of Toto, climbs off the bed… and walks forward, looking around her)* Toto… I've a feeling we're not in Kansas any more. We must be over the rainbow.

by L Frank Baum, adapted by LAMDA from the Warner Bros film

Crush

MARGIE is a little girl with a big crush on one of her classmates. Here she tells a friend why she likes Marcus so much.

MARGIE: Can you see him? He's over there. There. Next to Jacqueline. – Jacqueline Mason. My best friend. – No! Don't stare at him! He'll see you're looking.

(She gets sweets out of her pocket)

Do you want a sweet? He gave them to me yesterday, but I'll let you have one. Just one. – No! One! – Put that one back. I saw you. – I'm going to keep at least one of them for ever. As a keepsake.

(She puts the sweets back in her pocket)

I love Marcus Jordaine. He's so lovely. He has very straight teeth – except for that gap at the front. But his second teeth will be coming in very soon, so he won't look like a letter-box any more. And he's got ever such pretty hair – all curly like a mop.

(She gets out a Valentine's card and shows it to the audience)

I also love him because he's kind. Look. He gave me this. We had to make them in class yesterday and I was having trouble sticking the hearts on, so he helped me. When we'd finished them, the teacher said we could either take them home or give them to someone in the class that we liked. Horrible Ian Turton gave his to Samantha Fellows, saying she ought to keep it as it was prettier than she was. But she got him back at playtime. She rubbed about six Jammie Dodgers into his hair. The teacher went mad at both of them.

(She looks lovingly at the card)

But Marcus just walked up to me with his card – in front of the whole class – and said I was very nice and he wanted me to have his card. The class all giggled – but I didn't care. – I'm putting it away now in case it rains. I don't want it getting smudged.

(She puts card away)

by Ann Cartwright

All I Want Is Scruffy Back

Scruffy is a dog whose owner, SAM, is upset because he has gone. Sam's parents never liked Scruffy and it looks as though they know why the dog has gone missing.

SAM: He wouldn't just wander off, not Scruffy… Mum didn't like him the minute I brought him home. "Nasty, scruffy little mongrel," she said… "Dogs smell the place up," she said. I suppose from the very beginning I should have known she had it in for him. "Get that dog off your bed," she'd say, "he's got fleas." But he didn't really, except for one or two, and what's one or two on a dog that's part Labrador and part Irish Setter? Nothing. Then when he started stealing things… You see, he was so big, he could rest his head on the dinner table. One Sunday I saw him lick the entire joint of lamb, all over, while Mum was making the gravy, but I never said anything. We all ate it an' lived. But it was last Sunday that did it, when he munched up the entire chicken when Mum was mashing the potatoes… By the time she'd got through, all she found was a wing on the carpet behind the sofa. I didn't mind having just vegetables for dinner, but the others moaned a bit, and Mum was so hysterical she spent the rest of the day in bed. It must have been because while we were eating our mashed potatoes he went into the kitchen and ate the apple crumble.

I think Mum gave Dad an ultimatum… "It's either that dog or me!" Well, Dad took about three days to think about it… He's not the sort of man to act on impulse, or when he's being bossed… and Mum must have got a bit impatient. Yesterday she said he started having fits, frothing at the mouth he was (Scruffy I mean, not Dad). Mum said she got really frightened. "What if he bites somebody?" she said. "He'd kill somebody if he went into a mad fit." So now he's gone. When I came home from school, he wasn't there… Mum was, having a cup of tea, and smiling quietly to herself…

"Give us a kiss," she said. But I couldn't, I just couldn't.

All I want… is Scruffy back.

by Jeffrey Grenfell-Hill

Gingerbread

HANSEL and his sister Gretel have wandered into the forest near their home. They suddenly realise that they are lost. As it is getting very late, they settle down to spend the night in the forest – hoping that they will be able to find their way out in the morning, or that someone will come to look for them.

HANSEL: *(Waking up and looking across at his sister)* Gretel... Gretel...are you awake yet? *(Shaking her)* No... still fast asleep. You were very tired yesterday and I know how scared you were.

(Looking around him) It's still very dark in here, and the trees seem so tall... like giants' fingers pointing to the sky.

(Standing up slowly and stretching) I'm so stiff! I ache all over! *(listening to the silence)* It's so quiet too. I can hear you breathing, Gretel... and the odd rustle of leaves in the trees... but, nothing else at all. That seems so strange. I always expected forests to be full of insects, birds and animals. Father says that wolves live in the darkest, deepest part of the forest but I'm not afraid.

(Moving around the clearing) Now which way should we go? *(Noticing a small pathway)* There's a little track just ahead. *(Looking back to Gretel)* Still sleeping? Well, I won't be long.

(HANSEL tentatively pushes his way through the grass) This is not easy to follow. It's very overgrown but... *(stopping abruptly)* what an amazing smell! Where is it coming from? I can smell chocolate, liquorice, marzipan, peppermint, treacle and, best of all, gingerbread! I must be imagining things.

(He suddenly sees a small cottage made out of gingerbread in a clearing ahead, and runs towards it, calling out) Gretel... Gretel... come on! Over here! I've discovered a house! It's amazing! It's incredible! It's made of gingerbread!

Continued ▸

(He kneels down and greedily starts to break off part of a window frame and stuffs it into his mouth) Mmm! This tastes so good! It's gingerbread! The whole house is made of gingerbread! I'm not dreaming. It's true. I can smell it! I can taste it! Mmm! I was *so* hungry.

(Looking up, he sees an old lady peering down at him. Hansel quickly jumps to his feet)

Oh! Oh, I'm sorry. I didn't mean to start eating your house. It smelt so good… I just started to eat.

Traditional, adapted by LAMDA

The Wind in the Willows

BADGER, Mole and Rat are Mr Toad's best friends. They have been trying to keep him out of trouble for a long time, but he is constantly in trouble with motor-cars, caravans and other crazy escapades. Here, Badger outlines his plans to 'convert' Toad.

BADGER: Good morning, Rat! Good morning, Mole! This is a formal call, you fellows! Summer is here – so – the hour has come!

Whose hour, I hear you ask! Why, Toad's hour!

The hour of Toad! I said I would take him in hand as soon as the winter was well and truly over, and I am going to take him in hand – *(Pause)* – TODAY!! Now – I shall need you chaps to back me up – but I have a sound plan – and some very important news. May I – *(Sits down)*

This very morning, as I learnt last night from a trustworthy source, another new and exceptionally powerful motor-car will arrive at Toad Hall on approval or return. At this very moment, perhaps Toad is busily arraying himself in those singularly hideous habiliments so dear to him, which transform him from a (comparatively) good-looking Toad into an Object which throws any decent-minded animal that comes across it into a violent fit. We must be up and doing, ere it is too late. You two animals will accompany me instantly to Toad Hall, and the work of rescue shall be accomplished. We'll save the poor unhappy animal! We'll rescue him! We'll convert him! He'll be the most converted Toad that ever was before we've done with him!

Yes indeed, the hour has come! Gentlemen – follow me! Onwards!

by Kenneth Grahame, adapted by Vivien Heilbron

Sheer Genius

TOM is a young boy who is being brought up by his strict Aunt Polly. In this scene, he is not pleased that he has been told to whitewash the fence on a Saturday morning.

TOM: (Grumbling to himself) It's just not fair. It's a lovely morning. Just the day to go fishing! Look at that fence! Thirty yards and nine foot high! I'll never finish it.

(He picks up the long-handled brush, splashes it into the bucket, then puts it back again)

(Sitting down on the ground) I shall be the laughing stock of the town. I *must* try and find a way out of it.

(He empties out his pockets) I haven't even got enough things to trade! A marble... a broken toy... just trash! *(Smiling)* Wait a moment! I've got a plan... a really good plan! There's Ben Rogers now. I'll try it out on him.

(He leaps to his feet, picks up the brush and starts to whitewash the fence) Hmm... he's not even seen me yet. I like the look of the apple he's eating. A big, juicy one! Ah! He's seen me. Now, I'll pretend not to have seen him.

(Tom carries on carefully whitewashing the fence and then suddenly pretending to have just noticed him) Why, it's you Ben. I didn't notice! Are you going swimming? Work! You think I've got to work? This isn't work, it's really interesting and I like it! Does a boy get the chance to whitewash a fence every day? Just watch me and see what I mean. *(Tom carries on, pretending to concentrate very hard)* Do you want a go? No... no, I reckon it would hardly do. You see, Aunt Polly's very particular about this fence because it's on the street. It would have been different if it was the back fence... but, it's got to be done very carefully. I reckon there isn't one boy in a thousand – maybe two thousand – that could do it the way it's got to be done! Jim and Sid wanted to do it but she wouldn't let them. So, you see how I'm fixed! If you did tackle this fence and anything

happened to it… *(Pausing)* Well, I suppose I might let you… if you were to give me your apple. *(Ben bites it and gives him half)*... The whole of it! *(Tom takes it, gives up the brush and sits down on a barrel close by)*

(To himself) What a pushover! That was easy! I'll soon get it finished this way. I'll get all the boys wanting to take a turn *and* I'll get some treasures to keep as well!

(To Ben) Go on, Ben. Make sure it's nice and smooth!

(To himself, munching his newly acquired apple) Sheer genius!

by Mark Twain, adapted by LAMDA from Tom Sawyer

Lorna Doone

The story takes place in the late 17th century. John Ridd, a young farmer's boy, has been exploring on Exmoor and finds himself on land owned by a powerful outlaw family, the Doones. He slips and knocks himself out, falling down a slope. In this scene, he is found by LORNA DOONE, the young granddaughter of the head of the family. She rubs John's forehead tenderly with a dock-leaf and handkerchief, as he wakes up.

LORNA: Oh, I am so glad. You *are* alive. Now you will try to be better, won't you? What is your name? How did you come here? What are these wet things in this great bag? *(Looking inside)* Why, they are only fish. *(Looking down at his feet)* But how your feet are bleeding! Oh, I must tie them up for you. *(Tearing off her kerchief from around her neck)* And no shoes nor stockings! Is your mother very poor? *(Trying to bandage his feet with the kerchief)* I cannot bear to see your feet. Oh do stop wriggling so much. I will bind them very carefully. I will just try not to look at them!

(Pausing) I'm sorry, I do ask a lot of questions, don't I? I had better introduce myself. My name is Lorna *(whispering)* Lorna *Doone*. I thought you must have known it.

(She moves away from John and begins to cry softly) Do you know what they would do to us, if they found you here with me? They would kill us both outright, and bury us here by the water.

(Sadly) You ask me why? Because you have found the way up here, and they would never believe it. Now, please go; oh, please go. They will kill us both in a moment. I like you very much – very much indeed, and I will call you John if you like – because I *think* that is your name. Only please go! Hush! I can hear shouting… and it's getting closer. They're calling my name… I can't come with you. I have to stay. I will tell you what to do.

They are only looking for *me*. Nobody knows you are here… yet. You see that hole over there? The one in the rocks, behind the waterfall, where you slipped. *(Pointing towards the rocks)* Look! look! There is a way out from the top of it; they would kill me if they knew that I had told anyone about it. Oh, here they come. Go… go on, quickly! *(Whispering)* And mind you don't come again. It's too dangerous.

(John runs off as LORNA lies down on the grass and pretends to be asleep)

by R D Blackmore, adapted by LAMDA

Level 1 Acting

Grade 1 Duologue

Titles in Level 1 Acting: Grade 1 Duologue

The Hare and the Tortoise

This is the story of how a cocky HARE confronts a determined TORTOISE in a race. At the beginning of the scene Tortoise is alone in a woodland clearing. He is doing press-ups.

TORTOISE: *(Gasping)* Up… down… Up… down… Left leg up… left leg down… Right arm up… right arm down. Phew! This is hard work.

(HARE rushes in and sees TORTOISE)

HARE: Ha ha! You obviously can't see how ridiculous you look Tortoise! Press-ups! With your shape?

TORTOISE: *(Angrily)* That's the whole point, Hare. I am trying to improve my shape! That's why I am doing press-ups.

HARE: *(Still laughing)* But your feet are so small: your arms and legs so stubby! *(Gazing at himself)* Now mine are long and lithe. Look at you now. You are so slow and you have no stamina.

TORTOISE: *(Resuming the press-ups)* No stamina! We'll soon see about that! I might be slow but I get where I want to in the end.

HARE: Do you indeed? So, if I challenged you to a race, you would accept the challenge?

TORTOISE: *(Stopping)* Of course. And even though you can run faster than the wind, I really believe that I can beat you!

HARE: *(Doubling up with laughter and dancing around TORTOISE)* I could dance round you all the way and still win!

TORTOISE: *(Slyly)* Shall we race?

HARE: *(To himself)* I really can't believe I'm doing this. *(Looking around him and calling out, loudly)* Where are our witnesses? Mr Rabbit? Mr Fox? Come out from the bushes and make sure we do this properly. Where shall we run to? Your lair, Mr Fox? That's a fair distance. Tortoise? Good.

Continued ▸

(TORTOISE and HARE get themselves lined up)

Ready!

TORTOISE: Steady!

HARE: Go! *(He leaps out of sight)*

TORTOISE: He's off to a good start. But we'll see. He's all mouth! Now I may be slow and steady but I will win this race. You'll see!

(TORTOISE mimes very slow running movements on the spot – oblivious to whatever is going on around him)

HARE: *(Darting back into the clearing. He starts to mime very fast running movements, then glances over towards TORTOISE. He stops, creeps behind some tall bushes and crouches down)* Look at Tortoise. He's going about as fast as a tortoise can! It's pathetic! He can't see me here in these bushes. *(Looking around him)* I think I'll just take a quick nap, then I will make a sprint towards the finishing line... *(He yawns and lies back in the grass)* No problem at all... No... problem. *(He falls asleep in the sun)*

TORTOISE: *(Constantly moving in slow motion)* I wonder where Hare is now? I'm getting rather hot and sticky round the edge of my shell. Surely it can't be far to go now. When I reach Mr Fox's lair I'm going to have the biggest feast of buttercups you have ever seen. Just... got... to... keep going!

HARE: *(Waking up with a start and flicking his long ears)* Oh, my goodness! Tortoise has passed me. He's near the finishing line. I can't believe it! It's not possible! *(He leaps into action and tries to catch up with TORTOISE)*

TORTOISE: *(Looking around him and finally stopping, acknowledging applause from the other animals who have come to watch)* Phew! *(Gasping)* Mr Fox! Mr Rabbit! I've made it. I've won! *(Looking at HARE, running towards them)* There's Mr Hare coming up behind me. Well... well! It seems that 'plodding' can win a race after all!

HARE: *(Flinging himself over the finishing line)* Oh! I'm here at last. I must have got… er… lost.

TORTOISE: *(Holding out a hand)* Here! Give me your paw. Let's shake on it. I did win, but I'll share my prize with you. *(He grins, falls on the ground and begins to munch noisily)* Have some buttercups?

HARE: *(Turning away in disgust… both at himself, and at the food offered)* Urrrrrgh!

Traditional, adapted by LAMDA

The Graveyard Book

Nobody Owens, known to his friends as BOD, is a normal boy whose family has been murdered. Bod has escaped and lives in a graveyard where he is being raised by ghosts. He has been learning the alphabet from letters on gravestones. In this scene, he meets the little girl SCARLETT Amber Perkins for the first time.

SCARLETT: What're you doing?

BOD: *(Sticking out his tongue)* Nuffing. *(The face on the other side of the gorse bush crumples into a gargoyle, tongue sticking out, eyes popping)* That was good.

SCARLETT: I can make really good faces. Look at this one. *(She pushes her nose up with one finger, creases her mouth into a huge, satisfied smile, squinting her eyes and puffing out her cheeks)* Do you know what that was?

BOD: No.

SCARLETT: It was a pig, silly.

BOD: Oh. You mean, like P is for Pig?

SCARLETT: Of course like that. Hang on. *(She comes around the gorse bush and stands next to BOD, who gets to his feet)* How old are you? What are you doing here? Do you live here? What's your name?

BOD: I don't know.

SCARLETT: You don't know your name? Course you do. Everybody knows their own name. Fibber.

BOD: I know my name. And I know what I'm doing here. But I don't know the other thing you said.

SCARLETT: How old you are? Well what was you on your last birthday?

BOD: I never was.

SCARLETT: Everybody gets birthdays. You mean you never had cake or candles or stuff? *(BOD shakes his head)* Poor thing. I bet you're about my age. *(BOD nods enthusiastically)* My name is Scarlett Amber Perkins and I live in a flat. We haven't got a garden. I've come out with my mother. She's sitting on a bench at the bottom of the hill, reading a magazine. She told me to be back in half an hour, and not to get into any trouble or talk to strangers.

BOD: I'm a stranger.

SCARLETT: You're not. You're a little boy. And you're my friend. So you can't be a stranger.

BOD: *(Smiling)* I'm your friend.

SCARLETT: What's your name?

BOD: Bod. It's short for Nobody.

SCARLETT: *(Laughing)* Funny sort of name. What are you doing now?

BOD: ABCs. From the stones. I have to write them down.

SCARLETT: Can I do it with you?

BOD: Well… I don't really know. The gravestones are mine, aren't they? But it would be more fun doing them together… with a friend. Yes. Come on. Let's see how we get on. Some are really difficult. Let's copy some of the names from the tombstones.

SCARLETT: They're quite difficult words. P-A-R-G…

BOD: P-A-R-G-E-T-E-R. Look, S-A-R-A-H…

SCARLETT: What does P-A-C-E mean? It says 'IN PACE'.

BOD: That's Latin. It means 'Peace'.

SCARLETT: That's a nice word for here.

BOD: *(Hearing someone call out)* Who's that!

Continued ▸

SCARLETT: *(Thrusting the crayons and paper back at BOD)* I got to go. That's my mother, calling for me.

BOD: I'll see you next time. Won't I?

SCARLETT: Where do you live?

BOD: Here.

(SCARLETT runs off, leaving BOD looking after her)

by Neil Gaiman, adapted by LAMDA

Squeak and Maiow!

This tale from the Congo comes from a time when a CAT and a RAT lived together in harmony on a beautiful island. They weren't satisfied with the good life they had, however, and wanted more. In this scene, they leave the island together to explore the mainland.

(CAT and RAT go to down centre and sit next to each other, facing audience and making rowing motions)

CAT: This manioc root makes a good boat, Rat.

RAT: You bet. It's sturdy and tastes good!

CAT: Hmmm, that reminds me… I'm hungry. What do we have to eat?

RAT: *(Looks behind himself)* Let's see… we have… uhhhh… we have…

CAT: I'm sure hungry!

RAT: Uhhhh… let's see… *(Looks desperately underneath himself)*

CAT: I'm really, really, *really* hungry! What's for supper?

RAT: Nothing. We apparently forgot to bring any food.

CAT: Apparently or actually?

RAT: Actually and completely. There is no food.

CAT: Ahhhh! We're in the middle of the ocean, miles away from land, and we have no food?

RAT: Well, if you want to put it *that* way…

CAT: How would *you* put it?

RAT: Basically, we're going to die. But don't panic.

Continued ▸

CAT: If we don't panic, what do we do?

RAT: *(Curls up on side)* I'm going to save my energy and go to sleep.

CAT: That's the best idea I've heard all day! *(Curls up on side, facing away from RAT)*

(CAT begins to snore. RAT rises on elbow and speaks to audience)

RAT: I just remembered something. This boat is made of manioc root. And manioc root is a food we Rats love very much. *(Looks at sleeping CAT, then audience)* Shhhhh! I'll just nibble a little bit from the bottom of the boat.

(RAT leans over and mimes nibbling floor; CAT awakes groggily and looks over at RAT, who pretends to be asleep)

CAT: Hmmm... I could swear I heard a very strange noise. Oh well...

(CAT lies back down and sleeps; RAT leans over and begins nibbling)

RAT: Oh, this is so delicious!

(CAT awakes a little quicker, looks over at RAT, who pretends to be asleep)

CAT: Where is that noise coming from? I must be delirious from hunger. Oh well...

(CAT lies back down and sleeps; RAT leans over and begins nibbling)

RAT: Oh, yum-yum-yum-yum-yum... just another little bite... whoops!

(RAT falls backward; CAT startles awake)

CAT: What's all the noise?

RAT: Noise? You mean the water rushing into the boat?

CAT: Water! Aiiieee! Where did *that* come from?

(CAT backs up, squats as if avoiding water)

RAT: It appears there is a hole in the bottom of the boat.

CAT: A hole! Where did *that* come from?

RAT: It appears someone's tooth has eaten a hole through the manioc root.

CAT: A tooth! And where did – *(Looks at RAT and suddenly comprehends)* You miserable, no-good, low-down –

RAT: Don't panic! This is not a time to panic!

CAT: Rat-faced...

RAT: Careful! I resemble that remark! Besides, this situation is not as bad as it looks.

CAT: Our situation? Let's review our situation. *You* talk me into leaving our island paradise, *you* forget to bring food, and – while *I* am starving – *you* eat a hole in our boat! Did I leave anything out?

RAT: Yes! We just sank! Swim for the shore!

(CAT and RAT roll over several times and mime swimming; they crawl back to down centre, panting)

by L E McCullough

Emily of New Moon

On Canada's Prince Edward Island in the 19th century, EMILY's father has recently died and she is an orphan. She has gone to live with her relatives on their farm, New Moon. At school, the girls have been teasing her mercilessly.

(RHODA and EMILY are standing with the other girls in the schoolyard)

RHODA: *(Sweetly, handing EMILY a box)* Here is a present for you.

EMILY: *(Taking the box and opening it, then flinging it away from her in horror)* A snake! It's a snake!

(The other girls, including RHODA, run away laughing. A moment later, RHODA turns and walks back to EMILY)

RHODA: Emily, I'm awfully sorry. I didn't know there was a snake in that box, cross my heart I didn't. The girls just told me it was a present for you. You're not mad at me, are you? Because I like you.

EMILY: *(A bit mistrustfully)* Really? You didn't know it was a snake? *(Shudders)* It was the nastiest thing anyone could have given me.

RHODA: *(Looking at EMILY appealingly)* Honestly, Emily. I really want us to be friends.

EMILY: *(Overcome by RHODA's sudden friendliness)* Well... well, of course we can be friends, then!

RHODA: I'm going to ask Miss Brownell to let you sit with me. I used to sit with Annie Gregg but she's moved away. You'd like to sit with me, wouldn't you?

EMILY: Of course, I'd love it.

RHODA: We OUGHT to sit together.

EMILY: What do you mean?

RHODA: *(Importantly)* We belong to the two best families in Blair Water, of course! If my father had his rights he would be on the throne of England.

EMILY: Your father would be on the throne of England! Why?

RHODA: We are descended from the kings of Scotland. So of course we don't associate with everybody. I take music lessons. Is your Aunt Elizabeth going to give you music lessons?

EMILY: I don't know.

RHODA: She ought to. She is very rich, isn't she?

EMILY: *(Defensively)* I don't know. I'm not sure you should ask me such questions, Rhoda.

RHODA: But we're friends now. We should tell each other everything. Your Aunt Elizabeth has an awful temper, hasn't she?

EMILY: *(Angrily)* No, she hasn't! Where did you hear that?

RHODA: Well, my mother told me that she nearly killed your Cousin Jimmy in one of her rages. Why doesn't your Aunt Laura get married? Hasn't she got an admirer?

EMILY: I don't know.

RHODA: *(Disappointed)* Well, I suppose you haven't been at New Moon long enough to find things out.

EMILY: No, I haven't. And it's quite different from what I've been used to. Everything changed when my father died.

RHODA: Your father was as poor as a church mouse, wasn't he?

EMILY: *(Deliberately)* My father was a very, VERY rich man.

RHODA: *(Staring in disbelief)* I thought he didn't have a cent.

EMILY: No, he didn't. But people can be rich without money.

RHODA: I don't see how.

Continued ▸

EMILY: No… most people don't understand.

RHODA: Well, you'll be rich some day, anyway – your Aunt Elizabeth will likely leave you all her money, Mother says. So I don't care if you ARE living on charity – I love you and I'm going to stick up for you.

by L M Montgomery, adapted by LAMDA

Apple Scramble

MARY and JUDY are walking home from school. Judy is feeling in the mood for something tasty to eat; Mary knows that this means trouble. It is late summer.

JUDY: Come on Mary. I only had that tasteless salad sandwich for lunch. *(Grimaces)* Nut and Lettuce. I can still feel the nuts in my teeth.

MARY: *(Sarcastically)* I suppose that couldn't be your fault. I mean, you didn't have to give up meat.

JUDY: Well, I felt sorry for that lamb in the advert. And I've been sponsored to give up meat for a month in aid of 'Veg For Life'. The problem is being in the school team for netball. I'm starving by 4 o'clock, but I'm sticking to the diet. That's why I need one of those. *(Points over a wall to an apple tree. Trying to persuade MARY)* Nice juicy apples. We'd only have to climb the wall. We did it yesterday.

MARY: It's private property. My brother told me that it belongs to grumpy old Ted Gilly and you know what he's like.

JUDY: But this isn't a normal field, it's got apple trees in it and apples just grow wild and… *(Moving closer to MARY, in a loud voice)* And I'm really hungry! Come on, don't be such a spoil sport.

MARY: Okay, but we've got to be quick. None of that: *(Putting on voice)* "Let's sit down and admire the countryside", like yesterday. I got home at half past five. Mum didn't believe me when I said I fell asleep under an apple tree.

JUDY: Come on. *(She scrambles over the wall)* Pass our bags. *(She does so. And checks to see if anyone's in the field)* All's clear.

(MARY climbs over the wall)

Continued ▸

MARY: Right, which tree today?

JUDY: *(Pointing)* This one. It's got the lowest branches. *(She jumps up trying to grab a branch. Stops to get her breath. Turning to MARY)* You're good at jumping. If you can grab the branch, I'll pick the apples.

(MARY tries a few jumps and finally makes a giant leap and grabs hold of a branch)

MARY: There, quickly Jude, it's heavy…

(JUDY takes ten apples off the branch)

Hurry, it's going…

(MARY's having trouble holding the branch. JUDY finally retrieves all ten apples)

JUDY: Okay. *(Standing back)*

(MARY lets go of the branch as it springs back)

(Pointing) Look, more have fallen off over there. Let's collect them. They'll do for school tomorrow.

(They get their school bags and together they fill bags)

MARY: They look good.

JUDY: *(Biting into one)* Hum… delicious.

MARY: *(Eating)* Mmm… yummy. Though my tummy was a bit odd this morning after yesterday's apples. Maybe eating four was a bit excessive, Judy.

JUDY: I had five. Never felt better. *(She lies back on the ground and relaxes)*

MARY: *(Looks at watch)* What time do you have to be home?

JUDY: *(In a sleepy state)* Soonish…

MARY: *(Relaxing)* It is lovely here – beautiful day – sunny. *(Looking into the distance she suddenly sees something)* What's that?

JUDY: What?

MARY: *(Pointing)* That.

JUDY: *(Sitting up)* Where? *(Looking shocked)* Oh… I think we'd better move, but very, very slowly.

MARY: Do you think it's…?

JUDY: No… *(Studying it)* It does look like… *(sudden panic)* it is! *(Collects bags)*

(They both make a dash for the wall)

MARY: He's moving.

(JUDY throws bags over the wall and climbs it. MARY tries to get a grip)

(Calling) He's charging! I wish I wasn't wearing red. *(She desperately tries to get a foothold. Finally managing to climb over. Collapsing on the other side)*

That's the last time we do that, okay?

JUDY: *(Nonchalantly)* Okay. *(Looking in bag)* I'll have enough apples to cover me until next Friday. Maybe we could nip back then. *(Looks at Mary, who scowls)*

MARY: Read my lips Jude, no!

JUDY: Right, well, I'll have to take up meat eating again. I quite fancy a roast beef sandwich actually… Mmm. *(Smiling)*

by Clare Price

The Twits

MR and MRS TWIT are a horrible couple who are constantly playing nasty practical jokes on each other because of their mutual hatred. In this scene, Mr Twit convinces Mrs Twit that she has 'the shrinks' and will soon disappear into nothingness.

MR TWIT: That stick's too long for you. *(Picking up the stick and examining it closely)*

MRS TWIT: Why so it is! *(Looking at the stick)* I've had a feeling there was something wrong but I couldn't for the life of me think what it was.

MR TWIT: There's something wrong all right.

MRS TWIT: What *can* have happened? *(Staring at her old walking stick)* It must suddenly have grown longer.

MR TWIT: Don't be a fool! How can a walking stick possibly grow longer? It's made of dead wood, isn't it? Dead wood can't grow.

MRS TWIT: Then what on earth has happened?

MR TWIT: It's not the stick, it's *you*! It's *you* that's getting *shorter*! I've been noticing it for some time now.

MRS TWIT: That's not true!

MR TWIT: You're shrinking, woman!

MRS TWIT: It's not possible!

MR TWIT: Oh yes it jolly well is. You're shrinking fast! You're shrinking *dangerously* fast! Why, you must have shrunk at least a foot in the last few days!

MRS TWIT: Never!

MR TWIT: Of course you have! Take a look at your stick, you old goat, and see how much you've shrunk in comparison! You've got the *shrinks*, that's what you've got! You've got the dreaded *shrinks*!

MRS TWIT: *(Begins to feel so trembly she has to sit down)* Aaaaagh!

MR TWIT: *(Shouting at his wife)* There you are! You're sitting in your old chair and you've shrunk so much your feet aren't even touching the ground!

(MRS TWIT looks down at her feet and they are not touching the ground)

Just look at you sitting there in your same old chair – you've shrunk so much your feet are dangling in the air!

MRS TWIT: Oh no! Ah! Help me!

MR TWIT: You've got the *shrinks*! *(Pointing his finger at her like a pistol)* You've got them badly! You've got the most terrible case of shrinks I've ever seen! I suppose you know what *happens* to you when you get the shrinks?

MRS TWIT: What? What happens?

MR TWIT: Your head shrinks into your neck... And your neck shrinks into your body... And your body shrinks into your legs... And your legs shrink into your feet. And in the end there's nothing left except a pair of shoes and a bundle of old clothes.

MRS TWIT: I can't bear it!

MR TWIT: It's a terrible disease. The worst in the world.

MRS TWIT: How long have I got? How long before I finish up as a bundle of old clothes and a pair of shoes?

MR TWIT: At the rate you're going, I'd say not more than ten or eleven days.

MRS TWIT: But isn't there *anything* we can do?

MR TWIT: There's only one cure for the shrinks.

MRS TWIT: Tell me! Oh, tell me quickly!

Continued ▸

MR TWIT: We'll have to hurry!

MRS TWIT: I'm ready. I'll hurry! I'll do anything you say!

MR TWIT: *(Giving her another grizzly grin)* You won't last long if you don't.

MRS TWIT: What is it I must do?

MR TWIT: *(Grabbing hold of MRS TWIT and starting to stretch her)* You've got to be *stretched*.

MRS TWIT: *(Screaming out in pain)* Aaah!

by Roald Dahl, adapted by LAMDA

Never the Bridesmaid

ROSIE is revelling in the description of a recent wedding at which she was a bridesmaid for the third time. She has dressed up in the bridesmaid's dress to impress JESSICA, her envious best friend, who yearns to be a bridesmaid.

ROSIE: I carried... *(walking sedately)* ... a basket of beautiful beautiful roses.

(JESSICA looks on longingly)

JESSICA: Oh! Rosie.

ROSIE: And I wore a circle of real flowers around my head on the day; like an angel's halo.

JESSICA: I've *always* longed to wear flowers in my hair, Rosie.

ROSIE: Everyone thought that the flowers were just 'me'. *(Pause)* Even the Bride said I looked as pretty as a picture.

JESSICA: Mummy said...

ROSIE: *(Cutting in)* I've been a bridesmaid three times already. So I know exactly what to do: I'm professional. *(Curtsying)* I wore pretty pretty almond pink wild silk the first time, white satin with lacy petticoats the next. *(Twirling around)* And this, last Saturday.

JESSICA: Mummy said...

ROSIE: *(Cutting in)* Jessica. You've *never ever* been chosen to be a bridesmaid, have you?

JESSICA: No! Not once.

ROSIE: Poor, poor Jessica. I feel *ever-so-sorry* for you. Really I do.

JESSICA: Mummy said the only reason that I hadn't was because...

Continued ▸

ROSIE: *(Cutting in)* Oh! Silly me! I haven't shown you my shoes yet. I almost forgot: how could I? *(Lifting skirt)* Look! Jessica. Cost-a-fortune. *(Pointing toes daintily)* But perfect with the dress.

JESSICA: Mummy said that the only reason that you're chosen to be a bridesmaid is...

ROSIE: *(Cutting in)* You're jealous! *Green* with envy. I've spent all this time telling you about the wedding because I thought you were interested because you're supposed to be my friend. It's hardly *my* fault that you've never ever been chosen. Is it?

(ROSIE sweeps off)

JESSICA: *(Shouting)* Rosie! Mummy said the reason you're so popular as a bridesmaid is because your Mother promises to write a massive cheque as a wedding present. *(Pause)* My Mummy calls it bribery. And says it's contemptible. *(To herself)* And gave *me* a lecture when I asked her to do the same for me. Just once: just the once: that's all I wanted. It's not fair.

(Stamping feet in temper)

by Heather Stephens

Extinct

JAMIE and JACK have been studying dinosaurs at school. They have been asked to work together to make a model dinosaur as part of their class project. Unfortunately, they are not very pleased at the idea of working with each other. In this scene, Jamie is sitting on the floor surrounded by books about dinosaurs.

JAMIE: *(Sulkily)* It's just not fair! I hate Jack Carter. He's so full of himself. Thinks he knows best... Miss Stephens is mean. She knows Jack will boss me around – like he does with all of us!

(Looking up) Here he comes now! Well, at least he's brought all the model making stuff.

JACK: *(Entering, carrying a pile of boxes. Crouching down next to JAMIE and putting all the model making kit on the floor)* Have we decided which one we're going to make?

JAMIE: *We* haven't decided anything yet.

JACK: Well, we'd better be quick. *(Pointing out pictures of various dinosaurs)* We could try a Stegosaurus. *(Looking closely at the book)* He's really interesting. Look at the armour on his body.

JAMIE: I thought they were thick spikes. We could make them with cardboard.

JACK: He had a small brain though, *(looking at JAMIE)* like someone else I know!

JAMIE: *(Picking up a roll of paper towel and hitting JACK over the head with it)* You watch out! I may not be brainy but I'm a good fighter!

JACK: Fighting! Typical! Now, *(pointing to another picture)* what about the Seismosaurus? He's massive.

Continued ▸

JAMIE: Too big! We couldn't make it in time. We haven't got enough stuff.

JACK: *(Playing around with the boxes)* You're right. He was 60 feet tall, 140 feet long and weighed 100 tons!

JAMIE: Sounds like Miss Stephens!

(The two boys look at each other and grin)

How do you know all that? Measurements and things. You sound like an encyclopaedia!

JACK: I didn't know it, silly! I was just reading it on this fact card. *(Holding up the picture)* Come on! You choose. We must hurry up.

JAMIE: *(Pointing to a picture)* That's the one! The Diplodocus. It says he had a long neck and a tail – with a thick body.

JACK: It says he was a vegetarian, could weigh as much as 50 tons and lived 150 million years ago!

JAMIE: Wow! *(Taking an armful of materials)* You do the body. I'll make the head and neck.

(The boys run around sticking the inside of a kitchen roll to a larger box. They continue to make the model during the rest of the conversation)

JACK: It's more difficult than I thought it would be.

JAMIE: It doesn't look at all like the picture.

JACK: We need something for the legs.

JAMIE: I've not made the head yet. *(He sticks a small ball on to the end of the 'neck')*

JACK: I don't know what to make the legs with.

JAMIE: *(Looking in the box)* Here's some plasticine.

JACK: That won't stick! Where's the glue?

JAMIE: You can't use glue with plasticine! Even I know that!

JACK: *(Passing small toilet roll centres to JAMIE)* Here we are! *(Triumphantly)* This should be better!

JAMIE: Come on. Give two to me! *(He sticks them on with sticky tape whilst JACK sticks on the other two legs. The boys jump up, stand back and admire their handiwork)* He doesn't look anything like the picture!

JACK: He's sort of lop-sided.

JAMIE: Where are the buttons? He hasn't got any eyes! *(Picking up a felt-tipped pen and drawing two eyes on the 'head')* Never mind – this will have to do!

JACK: *(Taking the pen from JAMIE and drawing beneath the 'eyes')* He's got a mouth now too.

JAMIE: I like him.

JACK: Even if no one else does!

JAMIE: *(Looking at JACK)* You know, I didn't want to work with you Jack – but I'm enjoying this.

JACK: So am I. Will you be my partner again?

JAMIE: Yes… yes, of course.

JACK: *(Looking at the model)* Let's give him a name.

JAMIE: *(Excitedly)* I know. How about 'Dippy'?

JACK: Dippy the Diplodocus. I like that. *(They both start chanting 'Dippy the Diplodocus… Dippy the Diplodocus')*

JAMIE: *(Unable to take his eyes off the model, whispering)* Jack. Look! Look at Dippy!

JACK: What now? It's time we told Miss Stephens that we're ready.

JAMIE: *(Insistently)* Look! He's… He's *moving*!

by Jacqueline Emery

Robots-R-Us Dot Com

A CUSTOMER phones the company that sold him a malfunctioning ROBOT.

CUSTOMER: *(Facing the audience as he speaks on his mobile phone)* Hello, is that Robots-R-Us Dot Com?

ROBOT: Malfunction… malfunction…

CUSTOMER: I'm calling about the robot you delivered today.

ROBOT: Emergency… emergency!

CUSTOMER: No, I'm not happy with him.

ROBOT: Disaster… disaster…

CUSTOMER: I know he's a sort of guard to keep the family safe but…

ROBOT: Man overboard… man overboard.

CUSTOMER: But he won't shut up.

ROBOT: Women and children first.

CUSTOMER: Of course I want to keep my family safe!

ROBOT: Red alert… red alert…

CUSTOMER: Some of his safety advice is just nonsense.

ROBOT: Hurricane approaching.

CUSTOMER: He's getting on my nerves and I would like you to come and take him back.

ROBOT: Batten down the hatches.

CUSTOMER: See, there he goes, talking nonsense again. Complete and utter tosh, if you ask me.

ROBOT: Mind the gap… mind the gap.

CUSTOMER: So when can you come and get him?

ROBOT: Level three... doors closing...

CUSTOMER: Of course he can't come to the phone.

ROBOT: *(Walks over and snatches the phone)* Hi Mick. It's Ronnie here.

CUSTOMER: What?

ROBOT: *(Speaking on the phone)* Yeah, I don't want to stay anyway.

CUSTOMER: You are a complete and utter phoney!

ROBOT: I had you fooled for a while though.

CUSTOMER: Ha, you didn't fool me for one minute. Now get out of here.

ROBOT: Okay, keep your hair on, I'm going.

CUSTOMER: And good riddance... Mind the step...

ROBOT: *(Trips over)* Ahhhhh! You should have warned me, sooner.

CUSTOMER: Oh, sorry about that, Ronnie. *(In mock robotic voice)* Mind the step... mind the step.

by Andrea Inglis

Waiting

This scene takes place on the side of a main road on which a VIP will be passing by in a cavalcade of cars (it can be the Queen, a President, a Prince or Princess, or a celebrity). The two schoolchildren, NICKY and TONI, have been waiting for some time and at this point are getting bored. They sit in a dejected manner holding flags, amongst a group of spectators.

NICKY: How long have we been here now?

TONI: Three and a half hours. Look! *(Showing the time)*

NICKY: That's ages isn't it?

TONI: Look, this is once in a lifetime Nicky, so don't moan. Wave your flag a bit, go on. *(TONI waves half-heartedly)* Like me.

NICKY: Your flag looks nicer than mine. Look at it.

TONI: Well my Mum bought mine, yours was made in class wasn't it? As a project for today.

NICKY: Yeah, and the glue will probably get unstuck. Just my luck. I would rather be in school doing Maths. This is boring. *Mega* boring.

TONI: *(Getting out some sweets)* Have a mint.

NICKY: A mint! A mint in July. This is jelly-baby weather.

TONI: It will take your mind off waiting. *(They both suck on a mint)*

NICKY: Thanks.

TONI: The weather doesn't look too good, does it?

NICKY: Don't say that, we haven't got our macs with us.

TONI: It's the summer, isn't it?

NICKY: *(Looking at someone in the crowd)* Hey! Look at that man in the red shirt. He looks as if he's up to something.

TONI: Like what?

NICKY: *(Shrugging)* I don't know… He might have a gun…

TONI: Don't be stupid. He looks all right to me. Anyway, he couldn't see straight to shoot anyone, he's cross-eyed!

NICKY: Don't be mean. *(They both are laughing and trying not to look at the man)*

TONI: Oh no! It's started to rain. *(Holds out a hand)*

NICKY: We'll get soaked.

TONI: Hold your flag over your head like me.

NICKY: But mine will fall to pieces in the rain.

TONI: No it won't!

NICKY: Yes it will! I told my Mum she should *buy* me one. A plastic flag would be better than this paper one…

TONI: Hey, look Nicky, something's happening. Wave your flag.

(They both wave their flags, calling out an appropriate name)

NICKY: *(Stopping the flag waving)* Hey Toni, that's not a VIP car, it's too small…

TONI: *(Dejected)* It's the advance guard.

NICKY: *(Putting flag over head)* It's raining even harder.

TONI: *(Also putting flag over head)* We'd be better off watching this at home on TV.

NICKY: You could be right.

(They sit down on the kerbside looking bored, with their flags over their heads)

Continued ▸

TONI: *(Suddenly jumping up)* Look! The Rolls-Royce is coming. Wave your flag now.

(They both wave their flags furiously, calling out an appropriate name. Their eye-lines suggest the swift passing of a VIP car)

NICKY: I didn't see a thing!

TONI: Was anyone in it?

NICKY: It was raining too hard…

TONI: The glass was all wet…

NICKY: And we're wet…

TONI: What a cheat!

NICKY: Come on, let's go home.

TONI: Well, we can tell our grandchildren we once saw _______________

NICKY: Yes! For two seconds flat. A moving shadow. Great! And look at my flag. It's about to fall apart…

TONI: Oh! Stop moaning Nicky. This is part of History…

NICKY: I'll tell you what, I could do without History. It's boring!

(They both mime passing through a crowd of spectators as they exit)

by Jeffrey Grenfell-Hill

Level 1 Acting

Grade 2 Solo

Titles in Level 1 Acting: Grade 2 Solo

Jane Eyre

JANE is a young orphan living in a loveless home. In this scene, she has been locked in 'the red room' in which her uncle died.

JANE: Let me out! Let me out! I won't say my prayers. I won't! I won't! I don't care if Miss Abbott is right and something bad does come down the chimney to take me away. I really wish it would, then I wouldn't have to live in this horrible house again. But… I don't think it will and I'm scared. Scared of this lonely, cold bedroom; scared of those shadows and those flickering lights.

Oh, my head is aching so much after that fall! It just isn't fair to lock me away in here. If Uncle Reed had been alive he would never have allowed them to be so hard and cruel to me. Oh, why did they do it? Why?

Oh! There's a light on the wall and it's moving towards me. Oh look, the shadows and the lights… they seem to be moving across the room. They're coming closer. They're closing in on me. Help! Help! Bessie! Aunt! I can't bear it any longer! Let me out! Let me out! Please open the door. Please take me out. Let me go to the nursery. I'm afraid. Let me hold your hand, Bessie. Please don't turn away from me. Oh aunt, have pity. Forgive me! I can't endure it. Let me be punished some other way.

by Charlotte Brontë, adapted by LAMDA

The Stepsister Speaks Out

Cinderella's ugly STEPSISTER bemoans the fact that, although she tries so hard, Cinderella is beautiful, good-natured and gets the prince in the end.

STEPSISTER: It isn't easy being the ugly stepsister. Everybody always feels so sorry for poor little Cinderella, but what about me? I deserve a little sympathy, too. Does *my* fairy godmother ever turn up with a magic wand? Does the prince ever dance with me at the ball? Not on your life. The best I can ever hope for with my pumpkins is a decent piece of pie. And as for the rats, well, rats are rats, with their sneaky eyes and skinny tails, nibbling and gnawing at the garbage. I never saw one yet who turned into a coachman.

If you ask me, that Cinderella is weird. Certainly, she isn't normal. Besides the fact that she has naturally curly hair and wears size 4½ shoes, she is so good-natured that it's downright sickening. If you had to dust and sweep and clean all day long, would you go around singing to the birds? Of course you wouldn't. No sensible person would.

A lot of people think I'm jealous of her. Maybe I am. And with good reason. I subsisted on seven hundred calories a day for three whole weeks before the ball. I did my leg-lift exercises faithfully. I got a perm and a facial and a manicure. I even bought a new gown. Blue velvet. Designer label. I mean, I was *ready*. *Princey*, I thought to myself, *here I come*!

And what happened? Little Cindy, who has never seen the inside of a health club in her life and who doesn't know the caloric difference between a carrot stick and a chocolate éclair, whips together a dress out of some old curtains from K-Mart, waltzes off to the ball and snags the prince.

It isn't fair!

It really isn't fair!

by Peg Kehret

Evil Cat

EVIL CAT rules the household with an iron paw, keeping the Mummy and Daddy slaves well trained. However, sometimes Mummy and Daddy need to be taught a few extra lessons. In this scene, Evil Cat tries to wake them up.

EVIL CAT: *(Stretching)* Ahhh… a new day has dawned. I needed that restful twelve hours of sleep. I've got big plans. Today is the day. The day I mobilize. The day I take over the world!

(Hopping off the chair and strolling down the hallway. Peering through an open door) Something's not right here. There they are – my human slaves. Looking so contented, sleeping so peacefully. All is not well in the Universe. Hmm… what can I do about this? I've got it. My old friend – the kitchen table!

(Starts jumping on and off the kitchen table with a 'thunking' sound) I know they're stirring now… they can see me in their darkest dreams, on the kitchen table! *(Continues jumping on and off the kitchen table)* Haha! Will they get up and check? *(Peers through the open door again)* Wait! They're moving but not getting up. *(Impatient sigh)* I must think of something else.

(Saunters over to the kitty litter box. Runs claws along the bottom with a terrible scratching sound) What… still nothing from the human slaves?! *(Hops out and starts picking at the carpet)* Surely the Mummy slave is now asking herself if I haven't found the toilet up to my standards, and if I'm using the carpet instead… the furry carpet, the one they call 'the bathmat'. *(Peers around the corner again)* The Mummy slave has her head up, listening. Can she run? Can she make it in time to save 'the bathmat'? Haha! There will be no peaceful sleeping now! *(Pause)* Wait… her head is falling back onto the pillow. How disappointing. She used to have such fire in her to save 'the bathmat'…

Continued ▸

(Walks back to the open door) Sometimes, just sometimes, I let them sleep. But today is not the day for mercy. It's the day to conquer the world! And it's time for the big guns. *(Circles around, looking for a good spot)* No, not here... this is cheap flooring... Back to the kitchen and the nice hardwood floor. *(Starts making terrible noises)* Hack! Ack hack hack ack! Bleeaaaccchhh! Ah, there it is. Toxic cat vomit. Guaranteed to dissolve wax in two seconds and stain hardwood in five. *(Pause)* And what do I hear? Yes, yes... running, screaming... She'd better watch where she's putting her feet... Oh dear! Hahaha!

(Blinks innocently) A fine start to the day. Look out world...!

by Christina Kosaki

Sir Gawain and the Green Knight

King Arthur and his Knights of the Round Table are feasting for Christmas when a mysterious, giant Green Knight bursts into their hall and challenges them all. He asks if anyone there is bold enough to stand up and strike him a blow – if they are willing to take a blow from him in a year's time. Angered by his insolence, King Arthur is ready to confront the Green Knight. But his nephew GAWAIN has other ideas.

GAWAIN: *(Addressing King Arthur)* My lord, give me the axe. This Green Knight has insulted us all! Who does he think he is? How dare he defy King Arthur – and with such a crazy challenge? One of your knights should defend the honour of the court. I'm ready to do it! I will strike him such a blow that he will never have a chance to return the favour, whether now, or in a year's time.

No, I'm not the strongest or the cleverest of your knights… but I haven't had the chance to prove myself yet. And if I die, well, it won't be the greatest loss… Everyone thinks of me as just 'King Arthur's nephew'. How can I become my own man if you don't give me this chance?

(Taking the axe from King Arthur and addressing the Green Knight) What did you say, sir Knight? *(Sarcastically)* Everything about you is so… green, even your voice, that I find you remarkably hard to understand. *(Pause)* You want to know my name? It may be the last thing you ever know. My name is Gawain, and in a year's time I will be ready for you – if you are ready. Where shall I find you? No, no, don't answer that. First things first – you want me to try and chop off your head! This is unbelievable. But I'll do it, and gladly.

(The Green Knight kneels down. GAWAIN raises the axe high and lets it fall) There, sir Knight! Your blood is remarkably red for such a green man! *(Jumping backwards in sudden shock. To himself)* What… what… He's standing up – with his own head in his hands! He's getting on his horse! This is sorcery. *(To the other knights*

Continued ▸

and ladies) I cut his head off! You saw it happen, didn't you? He's dead! How can this be possible? *(Falling silent as the Green Knight speaks)* Yes… yes, sir Knight. I'll be at the Green Chapel in a year's time. I won't fail you. I promise you that I will be there. *(Pause)* There he goes! Riding out of the hall on that green horse of his, carrying his own head…

(To himself, half-laughing) What have I done? This is absolutely crazy. Well, I wanted an adventure… But I wonder if it will cost me my life.

Traditional, adapted by LAMDA

Treasure Island

The story is set in a coastal town in Devon during the 18th century. JIM Hawkins' recently widowed mother owns the Admiral Benbow Inn. One of their lodgers , an old seaman called Billy Bones, dies after he was cursed during a visit from a blind beggar. While he is looking for money that was owed for the lodging, Jim finds an oilskin packet among Billy's possessions. Jim and his mother manage to hide from Blind Pew and the band of pirates who return, looking for it. In this scene, Jim takes the packet to Squire Trelawney and Doctor Livesey.

JIM: *(Excitedly, trying to push past the maid who has opened the door)* Dr Livesey? *(The Doctor appears, accompanied by Squire Trelawney)* I have brought you the packet, sir. Here it is. *(Stepping inside the Doctor's room and placing it ceremoniously on a table)* Shall I open it for you sir? *(He begins to open the packet)* It seems to contain a book and a sealed paper. Shall we look at the book, sir? *(Speaking aloud as he turns the pages)* There's some writing on the first page. Look at this. It's the same as the tattoo mark. It says, 'Billy Bones his fancy' – and there's another one – 'Mr W Bones, mate'. *(To the Doctor)* Perhaps it is like a diary. *(Looking at the book again)* I wonder what 'Off Palm Key he got it' means!

(Looking at Squire Trelawney) Squire Trelawney, I wonder who 'got it' – and what 'it' was that he got. A knife in his back as like as not. *(Continuing to look through it)* I cannot understand this part at all. *(Looking up)* It doesn't make any sense. *(Looking at the book again)* Sometimes a place name appears to have been added – like 'Off Caracas'. *(Flicking through the rest of the pages)* I think this covers about 20 years – and right at the end there is a much altered 'grand total' and the words 'Bones his pile'. *(Looking at Squire Trelawney)* You were right all along sir. We have found his account book!

Continued ▸

(Looking at the second packet and opening it carefully) I can't believe our luck! Look. Here is a map of an island – with latitude and longitude, soundings, names of hills and inlets – and every particular that would be needed to bring a ship to safe anchorage. It looks like a fat dragon standing up. *(Peering closer to examine the map)* It's got something written in the middle – let me see – it says 'The Spy-glass'. There are also three crosses in red ink – two in the north, one in the south-west – and – oh, Dr Livesey, it says 'Bulk of treasure here'. *(Excitedly)* That's in different handwriting! We've found the treasure-map! You'll be rich!

by Robert Louis Stevenson, adapted by LAMDA

Where My Wellies Take Me

PIPPA is a young girl spending her holidays with her Aunty Peggy in the Devon countryside during the 1950s. In this scene, she is reflecting on the things she likes about the countryside, while imagining herself taking part in the annual May Day race.

PIPPA: I'm not mad about games and I hate races, so yes, I would miss the whole horrible thing if I could... But I know enough not to say it out loud... Walking is different though. My wellies like to go for a walk and I just go with them! I put them on... and I'm off!

(Looking around her) The whole world smells new. *(Moving carefully, but almost slipping over)* Ooops! The cobbled path to the churchyard is slippy with moss, so you have to be careful. I like to go past Annie's grave and touch her gravestone.

(Crouching down, pushing the foliage back and reading)

'Here lies Annie Bisset, who
passed away, aged 8
on 15 May 1887
Gone, but never forgotten.'

She was exactly my age. That's why I touch the stone, so she knows I haven't forgotten.

(Moving away from the gravestone) The quickest way out of the churchyard is to slide down the bank into the lane. Even if it does give me a wet backside – it is the best way. *(Looking towards a stream)* We're in Marsh Field now. There's millions of cowpats in Marsh Field. Dry ones, hard-baked, so hard that you could pick one up and throw it like a discus. Just like this. *(She stoops to pick one up, attempts to throw it, but drops it in disgust)* Urgghhh! That one is still wet and definitely not hard-baked enough. *(Running to the stream)* I must wash it off. My fingers are covered in gunk... and it stinks like anything! One thing's for sure, I won't do discus throwing with cowpats ever again.

Continued ▸

(Looking around her) What's that sound? I can hear the Church bells ringing… and they shouldn't be. It's not Sunday is it? And there's music playing too, the silver band, and look, there's flags flying everywhere. *(Excitedly)* The race… I've been in my own world and forgotten, the Round the Island Road race, all three miles of it. But look, *(beginning to run on the spot)* the finishing tape's right there ahead of me and they're all cheering me on… the whole village! I'm running now, and funnily enough I'm not puffed and my legs don't hurt at all. I'm going for the finishing tape, arms raised like an Olympic champion, an Olympic champion in wellies…!

by Clare and Michael Morpurgo, adapted by LAMDA

The Hundred and One Dalmatians

The wicked CRUELLA DE VIL loves Dalmatian dogs – because she thinks their skins make lovely coats. She has kidnapped the Dearlys' beautiful puppies, along with other Dalmatians. Here, she makes plans for disposing of all the puppies.

CRUELLA DE VIL: Saul! Jasper! Turn off that television. And turn on the lights. And turn the sound right down. I have something to talk to you about my lads. Tonight, the dogs must be killed tonight.

Yes I know we were going to wait until they were bigger Jasper, but some of them are, the older puppies, and the smaller ones can be made into gloves. Anyway, that's not the point. The point is, they must be killed before anyone finds them. There's been too much in the newspapers at the moment. They'll even be on the television news tomorrow morning. All England's looking for the Dearlys' lost puppies.

Kill the Dearlys' puppies and let the rest grow until they're big enough? What a stupid suggestion Saul. How on earth can we tell which are the Dearlys'? Have they got different spots or something? Can you really tell the difference?

Someone's bound to hear them barking and tell the police. I've told my husband. He's going to ship the skins abroad. I'll be keeping a few for my own coat. I've decided to make the coat reversible. Baby Seal on the inside, and Dalmatian on the outside.

These puppies must be got rid of quickly.

How? I don't care how. Stand on them, smother them, drop them off the roof. Have you got any gas, or chloroform? There are lots of lovely ways to do the job. If I had time, I'd do it myself.

Yes, I know I'd do it beautifully Jasper. You could watch. It would be such a pleasure for you. You could learn from an expert. I am sorely tempted. No, I have to get back to London.

Continued ▸

After you have killed them, they must be skinned immediately. And we will be counting the bodies. If you have let even one of the 99 puppies escape I'll throw you out of Hell Hall.

Goodnight, and Goodbye you horrible little beasts. You'll be so much improved as skins. And I can't wait until you're made into my own special coat. I'm really looking forward to that!

by Dodie Smith, adapted by LAMDA

Evacuee

During World War Two, children from London were evacuated to safer areas of the country to avoid the danger of the air raids. PAULETTE is a young, confused child who is about to leave her family to travel to the countryside.

PAULETTE: Where am I going? Why am I going? Do I have to go? I don't want to leave! What is happening?

(Pause) Have I got everything? My mac, hat, suitcase, gas mask and teddy.

(Pause) Mum took me to the station and she cried all of the way so I cried.
"If we are so unhappy then why am I going?"
"It's safer," Mum said, "you'll be away from the air raids."
She smiled and touched my face and looked deep into my eyes.
"You'll have lots of new friends, lovely fresh air and you can enjoy the countryside."
The countryside?
"What will the countryside look like?"
"Like a great big park," she said, "with trees and sheep and cattle."
We stood there on the platform, together, waiting. But waiting for what?
"Time to go," Mum said and we all boarded the train and waved goodbye.
I looked out of the window for as long as I could until Mum was just a dot left standing on the station platform.
The train was hot and sticky. Children everywhere, laughing, playing and crying.
Lots of crying all the way to the countryside.

(Pause) "Off the train!"

(Pause) People came and just looked at us.

Continued ▸

(Pause) What were they doing? They took some of the children away. But nobody wanted me until Mrs Smith. A big fierce-looking lady in an apron and curlers.

"Rules!" she said in a gruff tone.

> "No evacuee can use the front door!
> No evacuee can use the front parlour!
> Evacuees must eat their meals in the kitchen.
> Evacuees must share a bed.
> Evacuees must be in by 6 pm.
> Evacuees must be grateful for a roof over their heads."

Grateful? This is a nightmare and I can't wake up.

(Pause) When can I go home?

(Pause) Please! I just want to go home.

by Jenny Thornton

A Touch of Gold

The scene takes place when Greece was the centre of the Universe and Greek gods and goddesses ruled kingdoms through their immense powers. There was once a king called MIDAS who was greedy to become the richest man on earth. The gods decided to grant his wish but with disastrous consequences. In this scene, Midas is sitting on a golden throne in his garden of statues. He is suddenly aware that he is no longer alone. He looks up and notices Jason, a young boy from the village, who has broken into the palace to find out if the rumours he has heard about his king are true.

MIDAS: Hello! What are you doing here in my private garden? Snooping, I suppose? I'm surprised that you got past my guards but, well – I'm a little short-staffed at the moment. I wish you'd stop looking at me like that – mouth open! Have you never seen a king before? Well… no, you probably haven't. *(Looking around him)* Certainly not such a rich one!

(Getting up) Let me show you around. This is my palace… my swimming pool… my, er, statues. Yes, I do have a lot and yes, they are all gold… solid gold! My robes are gold thread, my throne is gold, my goblet is gold.

(Coming closer, and moving towards Jason) Shall I let you into a secret? I love making money… lots of it. My own little empire! One day, though, I made a wish which I have rather regretted. I wished that everything I touched would turn to gold. The gods heard me and granted my wish! *(Midas sees a coin lying on the ground and picks it up)* Look! It was copper… but now… it's gold! *(He plucks a flower from a bush)* This flower – see, it's now gold leaf! I can't even pick up bread or cheese because if I did it would turn to gold.

Continued ▸

No... don't back away. Are you getting nervous? Afraid that I might accidentally touch you? *(Moving towards the statues by the pool)* This statue of a dog – it wasn't always a statue, it was Hellen, my favourite hound, and these guards, yes, they were once living, breathing men! *(Turning towards the statue of a beautiful girl)* This is the worst of all! She was so beautiful, so full of life. Her name was Zoe. She loved to laugh and run and sing and play the lyre. *(Sadly)* She was my daughter. I just touched her like this *(putting his hand out)* and she turned to gold! No more laughter... no more songs.

Oh dear! Don't be afraid! Just be careful what you wish for... *(He reaches out to put his hand on Jason's arm)* Mmm. Too late, I fear. I seem to have gained another statue!

Traditional, adapted by LAMDA

A Terrible Tomboy

The story takes place during the early 20th century. Accustomed to a daily account of the doings of both himself and his classmates, Peggy has begun to realise that all is not well with her brother, BOBBY. Instead of being full of his usual fun on the homeward journey in the pony trap, he has scarcely anything to tell her. He has been late for several days at their meeting place, and has arrived looking so flustered that, although he has laughed it off and made some excuse, she is certain that things are not as they should be. The pair have never had any secrets before. Peggy waited at first for Bobby to tell her, but the confidence was not forthcoming. In this scene, Peggy asks Bobby what is wrong. Bobby finally decides to tell her.

BOBBY: What is wrong? Not much… but… well, *(plucking at the corners of his dog-eared Latin Grammar book)* if you really want to know, it's Jones Minor. I didn't mean to breathe a word, because I hate to be a sneak but, after all, telling you isn't like telling any of the fellows, is it? I mean, you are my sister. *(Quietly)* I hate Jones Minor. He lies in wait for me every afternoon, and I have to dodge everywhere to hide and get out of his way. I came round by five back streets today, and climbed over a garden wall. He's a bigger boy than me – about thirteen I think. *(Boldly)* If he were anywhere near my own size I'd fight him back. *(Angrily)* Jones is so mean though, and cruel. He doesn't fight properly, he pulls my ears, and bumps my head against the wall. He twists my arm round, too, and hammers at it. Do you know, he says he keeps a buckle-strap in his pocket specially for me. He's just generally a beast, that's what he is.

(Looking at his sister, sadly) If only Archie were at home. I haven't anyone else at school to champion me. I'm sorry Peggy, I didn't mean to whine to you about it. Don't you worry. I'm growing all the time, and perhaps one day I'll be big enough to go for him. I ought

Continued ▸

to be able to stand up to a bit of bullying. It goes on at school to lots of boys and not just me. It's always the older boys picking on the younger, smaller ones. Do you know, they took Holmes one day, and held him upside down with his head in the lavatory basin till he nearly choked, and they tied two others up as sparring-cocks today, and made them fight all dinner-time. It's only Jones Minor who bothers me. Still, when I think about it, he isn't as bad as some of the others – so I should be grateful for that! *(Smiling)* I wish you could catch him at it though! You would probably fight him just as well as Archie could. *(Laughing)* Can't you just imagine it, Peggy! The gossip all over Warford! Jones Minor has been knocked down and thrashed by a *girl*!

by Angela Brazil, adapted by LAMDA

Level 1 Acting

Grade 2 Duologue

Titles in Level 1 Acting: Grade 2 Duologue

The Amazing Maurice and His Educated Rodents

Maurice, a clever talking cat, has teamed up with a group of intelligent, educated rats and a flute-playing boy, Keith. In order to get rich by trickery, they go from town to town and invade as a 'plague' of rats. When Keith pretends to play the rats out of town with his flute, they all share the money he earns. They have had a few narrow escapes, so they decide to go into one last town and share the rewards. In this scene, two of the rats, DARKTAN and NOURISHING, are working underground for the Trap Disposal Squad.

(Follow spot on DARKTAN, as he makes his way along the tunnel)

DARKTAN: That showed them! That showed them what a rat can do!

(He exits. There is a loud 'snap' and a cry of pain from DARKTAN. A moment's pause, then NOURISHING rushes on)

NOURISHING: Darktan? Darktan!

(A groan from DARKTAN, off. NOURISHING crosses to him and looks to where he lies, offstage)

You're caught in a trap!

DARKTAN: *(Off, forcing out some heavy sarcasm, despite the pain)* Oh… really?

NOURISHING: I'll go and fetch Sardines, shall I?

DARKTAN: *(Off, with effort)* No! Tell me… what… kind… of… trap?

NOURISHING: Er… er… er…

DARKTAN: *(Off) Think*, you miserable widdler!

Continued ▸

NOURISHING: Er, er, it's all rusty. Rust everywhere. Looks like it could be a Breakback – yes, there's a bit of the sign – it's a... Nugent Brothers 'Breakback' Mark 1, sir!

DARKTAN: *(Off)* That's ancient, that is! Can you see how... can... you see how... the spring, the spring... So – this is how it happens. Perhaps there really is a Big Rat, deep underground... The Bone Rat... nothing to fear... just walk into the light, Darktan... it's so easy...

NOURISHING: It's all rusted, sir!

(She moves into the wing. There is a grinding sound)

(Off) I've gnawed through it, sir! It's old and weak!

(She comes on, helping DARKTAN, who has a red mark around his waist)

Probably why you weren't cut in half, sir! Can you hear me, sir?

(She helps DARKTAN to the ground)

DARKTAN: *(Dreamily)* Quite nice, really. This must be where the Big Rat lives...

NOURISHING: Darktan, sir? I gnawed right through the spring, sir...

DARKTAN: He must know a lot, the Big Rat.

(He passes out)

NOURISHING: Sir? Sir? Are you still dead, sir? Sir?

(A small pause, and then DARKTAN breathes in, painfully and noisily)

It's amazing! You were dead in the trap and now you're alive!

DARKTAN: Nourishing? I'm very grateful, but don't get silly. The spring was stretched and weak and the teeth were all rusted and blunt. That's all.

NOURISHING: But there's teeth marks all around you! No one's ever come out of a trap before!

DARKTAN: I was just lucky.

NOURISHING: Did you see the Big Rat?

DARKTAN: What? No, well, I'm not actually sure. There was a light and… is Hamnpork all right?

NOURISHING: Sort of. I mean, we can't see any wounds that won't heal. He's had worse. But he was pretty old. Nearly three years.

DARKTAN: Was?

NOURISHING: *Is* pretty old, I mean, sir. Sardines sent me back to find you because we need you to help us to get him back, but –

DARKTAN: I'm all right. I'm sure it looks nastier than it is. Let's get up there then, shall we?

(Black out)

by Terry Pratchett, adapted by Stephen Briggs

Penalty!

Two football players, the GOALIE and the STRIKER, have clashed and are getting up.

GOALIE: That was never a penalty. Never!

STRIKER: Good one, ref.

GOALIE: How can you give that?

STRIKER: Looked clear to me.

GOALIE: Clear? But you –

STRIKER: Ref's decision.

GOALIE: You know it wasn't. If you score now…

STRIKER: *When* I score –

GOALIE: It'll be a travesty.

STRIKER: It'll be 2-1.

GOALIE: How can you stand there and –

STRIKER: Get back on your line. Ref!

GOALIE: OK, OK, I'm going back. But that was no foul.

STRIKER: I've got stud marks down my shin. Look!

GOALIE: They're days old.

STRIKER: Ref, he's nowhere near his line.

GOALIE: I'm on the line. See – line. This could lose us the championship.

STRIKER: Championship? No chance!

GOALIE: OK, I'm ready. But that was no foul. No way. You'll miss anyway.

STRIKER: I could stick this past you with my eyes shut.

GOALIE: Try it, hot shot! Come on, try!

(The shot is saved)

Yes! Not so cocky now, eh?

STRIKER: Ref, he came forward!

GOALIE: Ref, you can't. I moved sideways, that's all.

STRIKER: You came off your line.

GOALIE: A side-step, that's all. Oh, ref!

STRIKER: Yes, ref! Nice one. Give us the ball.

GOALIE: You can't be serious.

(STRIKER snatches the ball from him. They both look round)

What's happened?

STRIKER: The lights have failed. Can't see a thing. What happens now? Ref, you can't. You can't abandon it. There's only a minute left. We're just about to win.

GOALIE: *(Approaching)* Not with your shooting, peg-leg.

STRIKER: Come here and say that.

(They clash and roll around the floor. The lights come back on. They stop)

The lights are back on.

(Both look up at the ref)

GOALIE: Hi, ref.

STRIKER: Er, just putting some divots back. Oh no, ref, not red.

GOALIE: Ref!

(Both up)

Continued ▸

STRIKER: Off? Both of us?

GOALIE: He started it.

STRIKER: It was him.

(They slowly go off)

GOALIE: If you hadn't dived.

STRIKER: You brought me down.

GOALIE: No I didn't.

STRIKER: Yes you did.

GOALIE: I never touched you.

STRIKER: You nearly broke my leg.

GOALIE: I wish I had.

by Clifford Jury

Unicorns and Alley Cats

On a rainy night in a big, busy city, DUDE the alley cat and KIM the unicorn meet and talk about their lives. Dude is an experienced city dweller, while Kim comes from a faraway land and is frightened by the noise and bustle of the city.

DUDE: Ah, rain. *(Smiling and stretching)* What a wonderful thing it is. So refreshing… *(Jumps down and splashes a puddle with his paw and shakes it off. He jumps through another mud puddle)* I love puddles. *(Takes a deep breath and then coughs a little)* The smells of the city that the rain brings out are unequalled. *(Smiles and looks around)* I love the city. *(Calls out)* What would I do without you?! *(Yowls loudly, a window slams shut. Smiles and chuckles)* This is great!

(Suddenly, the sounds of loud honking and cars slamming on their brakes are heard from the street. DUDE is startled and hops behind his box. He peeks out from behind it just as a unicorn, KIM, runs into the alley and stops, out of breath and very scared)

KIM: *(Panicked)* Oh, why did I ever come here? This is a perfectly awful place. *(DUDE moves around the box in awe at seeing a unicorn)* It's smelly, rainy and dirty. The people are so unkind. Everything is so big. I don't understand it at all. I'm so very frightened. I want to go home.

DUDE: *(From behind her)* You're a unicorn!

KIM: *(Jumps back, scared)* Blaaah! What do you want?!

DUDE: Take it easy. I've just never seen a unicorn before.

KIM: *(Still scared and on guard)* I've never seen whatever you are before either.

Continued ▸

DUDE: *(Proudly)* I'm a cat. An alley cat to be exact. *(Picks up a newspaper off the ground and holds it up)* I have the papers to prove it. *(KIM tries to smile)* They call me Dude.

KIM: Dude?

DUDE: Actually, my birth name is Sir Douglas Paramount, but all my friends nicknamed me Dude. Easier to say, I suppose. What's your name, my fine horned friend?

KIM: Kim. Kim of the Jagged Peaks.

DUDE: Impressive. So where is this Jagged Peaks place?

KIM: Hidden in a land far away. It's not at all like this place.

DUDE: Ah, yes. The city. You like it?

KIM: To be honest, not really.

DUDE: Then why did you come here?

KIM: *(Relaxing a little, looks around)* I'm not sure.

DUDE: I'm afraid I don't understand.

KIM: I really didn't want to come here, but all unicorns must when they reach a certain age. Coming here makes you appreciate your home much more and realise how wonderful it really is. *(Memories of home make her sad)*

DUDE: I know what you mean. I once got lost in a park. I was so happy to get back to my alley. *(Jumps up on his box and smiles)*

KIM: *(Walks about and looks around)* Everything is so big and so close together in the city. *(Hugging herself)* I feel as if I'm being crushed. And the noise… *(She shudders)*

DUDE: *(Going to her)* Take it easy, okay. It's not so bad once you get used to it. The city is exciting.

KIM: *(Looking fearfully at the street)* I don't like exciting.

DUDE: *(Kindly)* Then go home.

KIM: I can't. The problem is, I don't know what's best for me.

DUDE: While you're deciding, why don't you enjoy yourself a little?

KIM: *(Not seeing anything enjoyable)* How?

DUDE: *(Jumping through mud puddles)* Try jumping and splashing through puddles. It's great fun.

KIM: I'm wet enough, thank you.

DUDE: You could go down to the market and beg for fish.

KIM: *(In distaste)* Fish?

DUDE: *(Trying to think of something)* You could sneak into a mattress store and sleep away the afternoon… *(chuckles)* … or at least until you're caught. *(Looks at her and sees she isn't responding)* No, I guess not. *(Thinks)* I know a great spot that overlooks the city. You can also watch the sunset.

KIM: *(Smiles a little)* That sounds nice.

DUDE: *(Excited)* Yes! A breakthrough! *(KIM smiles)* There's always the park and the duck pond is fun.

KIM: The park might be a good idea.

DUDE: See. There's something.

KIM: *(Sadly)* But, it's not home. *(DUDE sits in frustration and plops his face down on the ground)* I'll try harder. I'm sure I can like it if I give it a chance. I'm sorry. I don't mean to tell you all my troubles. I do feel better after talking to you.

DUDE: Good. I'm glad to be of service. *(Hops up on his box)*

KIM: Will you stay and keep me company?

DUDE: Can't. Gotta go.

KIM: What? You're leaving?

DUDE: Got places to go, rubbish bins to meet…

KIM: But, I'll be lonely again.

Continued ▸

DUDE: I promise you I'll visit every chance I get. *(He starts to exit)*

KIM: Bye.

DUDE: See you soon.

(He exits. Only the sounds of the city are heard. KIM is alone. After watching DUDE go she looks around sadly at the city. Then, she sees a mud puddle in front of her)

KIM: Puddles. *(Playfully she splashes through them and skips happily off)*

by D M Larson

Pollyanna

POLLYANNA's story takes place around 100 years ago. She is a young orphan who has gone to live with her stern Aunt Polly in the American town of Beldingsville, Vermont. Pollyanna's philosophy of life is always to find something to be glad about, and this has a positive effect on the unhappy people around her. In this scene, Pollyanna meets JIMMY BEAN, another orphan who is looking for a home.

POLLYANNA: Hullo.

JIMMY BEAN: *(Glancing up but looking away again at once)* Hullo yourself.

POLLYANNA: Now you don't look as if you'd be glad even for calf's-foot jelly.

(JIMMY BEAN stirs restlessly, gives her a surprised look, and begins to whittle again at his stick. POLLYANNA hesitates, then drops herself comfortably down near him)

POLLYANNA: My name's Pollyanna Whittier. What's yours?

JIMMY BEAN: Jimmy Bean.

POLLYANNA: Good! Now we're introduced. I live at Miss Polly Harrington's house. Where do you live?

JIMMY BEAN: Nowhere.

POLLYANNA: Nowhere! Why, you can't do that – everybody lives somewhere.

JIMMY BEAN: Well, I don't – just now. I'm huntin' up a new place.

POLLYANNA: Oh! Where is it?

JIMMY BEAN: *(Looking at her with scornful eyes)* Silly! As if I'd be a-huntin' for it – if I knew!

Continued ▸

POLLYANNA: Where did you live before?

JIMMY BEAN: Why do you keep askin' questions?

POLLYANNA: I have to, else I couldn't find out a thing about you. If you'd talk more I wouldn't talk so much.

JIMMY BEAN: *(Giving a short laugh)* All right then – here goes! I'm Jimmy Bean, and I'm ten years old goin' on eleven. I come last year to live at the Orphan's Home, but they've got so many kids there ain't much room for me, an' I wasn't never wanted anyhow, I don't believe. So I've quit. I'm going to live somewhere else – but I ain't found the place yet. I'd *like* a home – just a common one, you know, with a mother in it, instead of a Matron. So I'm huntin' now. *(Voice breaks a little)* I've tried four houses, but – they didn't want me – though I said I expected to work, course. There! Is that all you want to know?

POLLYANNA: Why, what a shame! And didn't anybody want you? Oh dear! I know just how you feel, because after – after my father died, too, there wasn't anybody but the Ladies' Aid for me, until Aunt Polly said she'd take – *(Stops abruptly. The dawning of a wonderful idea begins to show in her face)* Oh, I know just the place for you! Aunt Polly will take you – I know she will! Didn't she take me? And didn't she take Fluffy and Buffy, when they didn't have anyone to love them, or any place to go? And they're only cats and dogs. Oh, come, I know Aunt Polly will take you! You don't know how good and kind she is.

JIMMY BEAN: *(His face brightens)* Would she, now? I'd work, you know, an' I'm real strong!

POLLYANNA: Of course she would! Why, my Aunt Polly is the nicest lady in the world. And there's rooms – heaps of 'em. *(Springing to her feet and tugging at his arm)* It's an awful big house. Maybe, though, maybe you'll have to sleep in the attic room. I did, at first. *(With a critical glance)* And you've got freckles, too, so you'll be glad there isn't any looking-glass; so you won't mind sleeping in that room at all, I'm sure.

JIMMY BEAN: I shouldn't think anybody who could talk like that would need to ask no question to fill up time with!

POLLYANNA: *(Laughing)* Well, anyhow, you can be glad of that, for when I'm talking, you don't have to! *(They run off toward the house, straight into the presence of her amazed aunt)* Oh, Aunt Polly! Just look here! I've got something ever so much nicer, even, than Fluffy and Buffy for you to bring up. It's a real live boy. This is Jimmy Bean, Aunt Polly.

by Eleanor H Porter, adapted by LAMDA

Best Friends

GEMMA and ALICE have been best friends since they were born. They see each other every day. It never seems to matter that Gemma loves football while Alice prefers drawing or that Gemma never stops talking while Alice is more likely to be listening. They share everything. Then one day Gemma finds out that there's something Alice isn't sharing – a secret. And when Gemma finally discovers what it is, she isn't sure if she and Alice can stay best friends for ever. In this scene, Gemma and Alice are crying after a disagreement with Gemma's mum, and Alice finally shares her secret.

ALICE: *(Handing GEMMA some kitchen towel to wipe her nose)* Gem. *(In a sad little whisper)* Gem, there *is* something to cry about.

GEMMA: I thought there might be.

ALICE: I don't know how to tell you.

GEMMA: *(Touching ALICE's lips trying to make her mouth move)* Just spit it out.

ALICE: *(After pretending to bite GEMMA's fingers)* I'm not very good at spitting. Unlike you.

(They giggle feebly through their tears)

GEMMA: Shall I spit it out for you? You don't want to be my best friend any more.

ALICE: *(Looking stricken)* No, it's not that!

GEMMA: It's OK. Well, it's not one *bit* OK, but I do understand. I'm not sure *I'd* want to be my best friend. I'm noisy and silly and messy and I break things and I get on everyone's nerves.

ALICE: You don't get on *my* nerves. I want you to be my best friend for ever and ever, only… only…

GEMMA: Only what? What *is* this great big secret, Alice? Come on, you've got to tell me.

ALICE: How do you know there's a secret?

GEMMA: Look, I'm ever so sorry and I know it's a totally sneaky thing to do and you really *won't* want to be friends with me now, but I read your diary. Just a line or two. Last night. Well, maybe I've had one or two peeps in the past but you never wrote anything *secret* before –

ALICE: Gem, stop burbling. *(Taking hold of GEMMA's hand)* I *do* still want to be friends. Though don't you dare read my diary again, you nosy pig. But I swore to my mum and dad that I wouldn't tell anyone, not even you, not till it was settled. But you'll find out soon enough anyway. The thing is, I think we're moving.

GEMMA: You're moving. Is that all? Oh Alice, that's OK. *Where* are you moving? Don't worry, if it's right the other side of town I'll get Dad to give me a lift to your new place in the taxi – it couldn't be simpler.

ALICE: We're moving to Scotland.

GEMMA: Scotland? But that's hundreds of miles away! But how will I see you?

ALICE: *(Crying)* I know, I know, it's so awful, isn't it.

GEMMA: What about school?

ALICE: *(Wailing)* I've got to go to a new school and I won't know anyone. I won't have any friends.

GEMMA: But *why* are you going?

ALICE: My Dad's getting a new job with this Scottish firm and my mum wants to live up there because we'll be able to get a bigger house. And we're going to have a huge garden and mum says I can have a swing and a tree house.

Continued ▸

GEMMA: *I'm* going to have a tree house, you know I am, when Dad gets round to it. It was going to be *our* tree house.

ALICE: And I can have any pets I want.

GEMMA: You've got a share of Barking Mad.

ALICE: Mum said I can maybe have my own pony.

GEMMA: *(Brought up short)* A pony! I've always longed for a pony. *(Staring at Alice)*

ALICE: It's still not definite we're going. So we're not telling anyone yet.

GEMMA: But I'm not *anyone*. I'm your best friend. *Why* did you keep it secret from me? I would have *had* to tell you or I'd burst! What are we going to do?

ALICE: *(Bitterly)* We can't do anything. We're just children. We don't count.

by Jacqueline Wilson, adapted by David Lawson Lean

Errol and the Ghost

Errol, an older teenage boy living in the Caribbean, has just started work in the nearest country town. He does not have any transport of his own and walks long distances at night, along country tracks, to return to his village. Every Friday evening his new, older workmates always invite him to join them in their local rum shop before he returns home. When he does arrive back he makes such a noise – whistling and singing, and crunching along with heavy footsteps – that he sets dogs barking and wakes up all his neighbours. They try to put him off walking along a certain path by telling him that it is haunted, but he takes no notice and continues to annoy everyone as usual. In this scene, two of his young cousins, MARSHALL and LEIGH, have decided to teach Errol a lesson.

(MARSHALL enters the alley at the back of the village houses and cautiously looks around to see if anyone else is there. He is carrying a pole and a bundle of material. LEIGH enters from the other direction, carrying a bag of flour and a bottle of rum. They meet in the middle)

MARSHALL: Psst! Leigh! *(Whispering)* Have you got everything we need?

LEIGH: Yes, I think so. I had a job getting the rum and the flour from the kitchen without being seen.

MARSHALL: Keep your voice down. We don't want to set the dogs barking. That would give us away.

LEIGH: Hey! This is going to be such fun. You know, little Pansy wanted to come too – but she got scared at the last minute.

MARSHALL: Of real ghosts?

LEIGH: No – just in case Errol catches us playing a trick on him. He won't like it one little bit!

Continued ▸

MARSHALL: Well, he shouldn't be so full of himself then! This will teach him to make such a noise coming home. All that whistling... and crunching of his boots! *(Both boys start to giggle)* Anyway, I'm glad Pansy stayed behind. She's just a little girl – and she'd only get in the way! Come on, let's start making this 'ghost'.

(The boys begin to make a figure, rather like a scarecrow)

LEIGH: Where shall we put it?

MARSHALL: It's got to be in a central spot where Errol will see it. *(He prances around with the pole, trying out different places)* What about... here?

LEIGH: No... it's too hidden.

MARSHALL: *(Changing its position)* Here?

LEIGH: No, that's too far back.

MARSHALL: *(Changing positions again)* Or here?

LEIGH: That's better.

MARSHALL: *(Pushing the pole into the ground)* Come on then... we'd better hurry. Give me the sheet.

(Leigh unties the bundle and, together, the two boys place the sheet over the pole)

LEIGH: Here's the hat! *(Proudly placing it on the 'ghost')*

MARSHALL: *(Giggling)* Where did you find that?

LEIGH: On the top of mother's wardrobe.

MARSHALL: It's her Sunday best, Leigh! We will be *killed* for this!

LEIGH: Will she find out?

MARSHALL: No. She might blame an intruder!

LEIGH: The same one who stole the bottle of rum...

MARSHALL: And the bag of flour...

LEIGH: And the sheets from the washing line!

(They both dissolve into laughter)

MARSHALL: Let's see if we can make the arms lean over so that our 'ghost' looks as if she is trying to gather someone up in them!

LEIGH: Urrrggghhh! That's so creepy!

MARSHALL: Well, we could try and tie some twigs on the arms so that, in the dark, they look like bony fingers.

(They adjust the 'ghost's' position and step back, admiring their work)

You know, they do say that this path is haunted anyway… by a real ghost!

LEIGH: It does go through the old family cemetery.

MARSHALL: Have you heard the story of the beautiful woman in white who has one real foot and one cow's hoof… and whose sweet smile makes anyone who sees her vanish forever?

LEIGH: Great story! But I don't think our 'ghost' looks particularly beautiful and she hasn't any feet at all! She can't smile either!

MARSHALL: *(Whispering)* What about the one about the big black and white dog which followed Mr Moombay when he went for the midwife on Good Friday night?

LEIGH: *(Shuddering)* I know that one. It's really scary. The baby was born dead the next morning.

MARSHALL & LEIGH: *(Together)* And the dog was never seen again!

MARSHALL: Well our 'ghost' isn't a dog either! It's just a kind of 'scarecrow ghost'. *(Looking around him)* Come on! Now, for the special effects! Are you ready?

LEIGH: *(Tearing open the bag of flour and sprinkling it on the 'ghost' and the path all around them)* First, the flour… that will look good. Nice and white in the moonlight.

Continued ▸

MARSHALL: *(Picking up the rum bottle and sprinkling rum all over the flour)* Here's the rum. This will make it 'glow' a bit and it smells good too!

LEIGH: *(Taking some black pepper out of his pocket)* I brought some black pepper as well. *(As he shakes it all over the path, both boys begin to sneeze uncontrollably)* It's fantastic! *(Sneeze)*

MARSHALL: Amazing! *(Sneeze)*

LEIGH: Really very 'ghostlike'! *(Sneeze... sneeze)*

MARSHALL: Listen! It's Errol... I can hear his boots on the pathway.

LEIGH: Quick! Let's hide!

(The two boys run behind a fence and crouch down behind it. They watch carefully as Errol approaches. As each boy tries to peer out, the other one pushes him back down again)

MARSHALL: *(Whispering)* Look at his face!

LEIGH: He's very scared.

MARSHALL: He thinks it's real! Ready for the sound effects? *(Whispering)* One... two... three.

MARSHALL & LEIGH: *(Together)* Whoooaaa! Whoooaaa! Whoooaaa!

by Pansy Griffith, adapted by LAMDA

There's Nothing To It

A CUSTOMER, impatient with the WAITER at a restaurant, suggests that they try switching places.

WAITER: Are you ready to order?

CUSTOMER: What's the soup of the day?

WAITER: It's water chestnut. It's the chef's speciality.

CUSTOMER: Water chestnut soup? What are the ingredients?

WAITER: I'm not sure really. Shall I ask?

CUSTOMER: No, never mind. Do you have any veal?

WAITER: Have you looked in the vegetarian section of the menu?

CUSTOMER: Veal is a kind of meat. Anyway, I haven't got a menu. You didn't bring me one.

WAITER: I'm sorry. You see I'm new to the job.

CUSTOMER: I never would have guessed.

WAITER: Yes. I only started this afternoon.

CUSTOMER: Well, you bring me the menu and I'll point to the things I want to order for my lunch.

WAITER: Great! Thanks. I'll just go and get one.

(WAITER exits and returns with a menu) Here you are. Enjoy your meal.

CUSTOMER: Thank you but you're meant to say that when you've brought the food.

WAITER: But you haven't ordered any.

CUSTOMER: That's because you've only just brought me the menu.

Continued ▸

WAITER: I haven't really got the hang of it yet. Sorry.

CUSTOMER: Look. You sit here and I'll be the waiter. You order something and I'll demonstrate what you are meant to do. There's nothing to it.

(They swap places)

WAITER: *(Looking at menu)* Waiter! Can you bring me a menu please?

CUSTOMER: You are holding a menu in your hands.

WAITER: This *(waving it in the air)* is a wine list. I cannot order food from a wine list can I?

(CUSTOMER exits then returns with a menu.)

CUSTOMER: Here we are. May I recommend the chef's Special Mixed Grill.

WAITER: No you may not. *(Gives the menu straight back)* I want egg and chips.

CUSTOMER: What?

WAITER: I said I want egg and chips. Are you deaf or stupid?

CUSTOMER: You can't speak to me like that. I'm a customer.

WAITER: No! I'm the customer and the customer is always right.

CUSTOMER: Look, we're only pretending. You're meant to look at the menu and choose something to eat. Then I take your order.

WAITER: *(Angry)* Do you want me to get the manager in here?

CUSTOMER: No, of course not.

WAITER: Then just get me the food I ordered.

CUSTOMER: But...

WAITER: GET ME MY MEAL NOW!

CUSTOMER: Sorry… yes. I'm going.

(CUSTOMER exits)

WAITER: She's right you know. There's nothing to it.

by Phil Jamieson

The Daring Game

HELEN and ELIZA are best friends at a girls' boarding school in Vancouver, Canada. Eliza is generally responsible and well-behaved, while Helen is wild and challenges authority. A few months earlier, the school's headmistress told the boarders that money had been stolen from the Pound Box, a collection box for the school. The thief was never found. Now, Eliza confronts Helen about the theft.

HELEN: Being in the school play is so much fun! I think the best part is that I get to drive you all crazy practising the songs every night. But I promise it will be worth it. *(Pause)* Eliza, you aren't even listening.

ELIZA: I know. It's just that... I have to ask you something. *(She takes a deep breath)* Did you take the Pound Money? *(Long pause)* I just have to know, Helen... that's all.

HELEN: Yeah... I took it. I'm the thief. Now I suppose you don't like me any more. Although I was only borrowing it, you know. I meant to pay it back all along. And I didn't think they'd find out so soon. They don't usually open up the box until the end of the year.

ELIZA: You could have been expelled or something. Weren't you scared when they found out that some of the money was gone?

HELEN: Well... sort of. *(Angrily)* But I stopped taking it before Christmas. I decided I never would again, and I won't. Do you believe me?

ELIZA: I would believe you... except for one thing. *(Pause)* Did you lie to me about stealing when you were younger? Remember when you told me that story?

HELEN: You mean, when I lived in Prince George? And I got caught with a bunch of kids who were stealing?

ELIZA: Yes. Were you actually stealing too? You didn't have to lie about that, you know.

HELEN: I didn't lie to you! I didn't steal then. I told you that! It just kind of gave me the idea for doing it last term, and for doing it... *(She trails off)*

ELIZA: Helen... what are you trying to say?

HELEN: *(Pause)* Listen, Eliza. Listen very carefully, because I never want to talk about this again. When I first came to Ashdown, I *felt* like a thief. My mother drilled it into me the whole time I was waiting to come here.

ELIZA: Because you got caught with those kids? I thought you were just tagging along. You said you didn't know what they were doing.

HELEN: I didn't. But my mother and stepfather made me feel so guilty. So when I came to Ashdown, I started taking things.

ELIZA: What kind of things?

HELEN: Just... little things, like people's china animals or comics. I returned them later. I just wanted to see if I could do it. It was *borrowing*, not stealing.

ELIZA: But why did you take the Pound Money? You didn't need it. You get pocket money like the rest of us. *(Pause)* Helen, sometimes I think you do things like that because you're bored.

HELEN: Yes, I was bored. And I *did* need it. I had no pocket money left the week we had the feast. And I had to bring something. My stingy parents wouldn't even give me money for my birthday, because my marks were so low.

ELIZA: Didn't you get *anything* for your birthday?

HELEN: Underwear.

ELIZA: What a ghastly present!

Continued ▸

HELEN: I know. So I took some money one more time. But I never will again. I've paid it back now, anyway. And I *never* stole with those kids. Now do you believe me?

ELIZA: *(Pause)* I believe you. I wish you had told me about the Pound Money. I could have helped you pay it back. But I suppose it was none of my business. I do believe you. I'm sorry I asked.

HELEN: Do you promise you'll never tell?

ELIZA: Of course I won't! You know that.

HELEN: *(Jumping up)* Let's go outside. It's not raining. Why are we wasting our time in here?

by Kit Pearson, adapted by LAMDA

You Can't Do That!

CORRY and ANDY are taking their first trip on an Underground or Metro train. They have managed to board the train as the doors close and are both out of breath.

(CORRY and ANDY sit side by side facing the audience)

CORRY: We only just squeezed in before the doors closed.

ANDY: You'd think they'd wait! It could be dangerous.

CORRY: It was bad enough coming down the escalators. All those people with luggage! Why don't they stand on one side?

ANDY: The trouble is, this train goes to the airport, so everyone has loads of luggage.

CORRY: Not everyone. Not quite, not us.

ANDY: Maybe not, but look around. You can hardly move in here.

CORRY: At least we got a seat.

ANDY: You wouldn't in the rush hour! *(Pause)* What are you looking at?

CORRY: I'm trying to read that man's newspaper.

ANDY: Oh! I see. Anything interesting?

CORRY: I don't know… he won't keep still.

ANDY: *(Looking around slowly then speaking quietly)* Everyone looks very miserable!

CORRY: Well! Wouldn't you if you had to be down here every day? No daylight!

ANDY: I'd hate it. Rattling around in a dark tunnel. I'd feel trapped.

Continued ▸

CORRY: I suppose it's quick. *(Pause)* Do you know, I've never been on one of these trains before?

ANDY: *(Amazed)* I thought you had. I could have sworn you said you'd done this before. You must have done! I was relying on you.

CORRY: No, honestly, this is the first time. Anyway, what do you mean, 'relying on me'?

ANDY: You know. I haven't been on one before.

CORRY: *(Puzzled)* But I thought... I was relying on you.

ANDY: For what?

CORRY: No wonder you didn't know what to do with your ticket.

ANDY: It's stopping. Not long between stops, is it?

CORRY: It's four stops before we need to get off.

(There is a long pause as the train stops at the station and then moves off. ANDY gradually becomes aware that CORRY is staring up at a fixed point above head height over the seat opposite)

ANDY: What's so interesting up there?

CORRY: I'm looking at a map of the line. Did you notice the name of that last station?

ANDY: Yes.

CORRY: Well, look up there. See the name of the station where we got on? *(Pointing)* There. *(ANDY nods)* Now look at where we've just stopped.

ANDY: *(Straining to follow)* Yes.

CORRY: Now, look for the station where we are going.

ANDY: *(With alarm) Oh, no!* We're going the wrong way!

CORRY: *(With a sense of panic)* What do we do?

ANDY: Stop the train!

CORRY: You can't do that!

ANDY: But *you* said this was the right train.

CORRY: Don't blame me. All we have to do is get off at the next stop and then go back the other way.

ANDY: You can't do that!

CORRY: Yes you can.

ANDY: *(Standing and looking around hopefully)* We'll have to ask someone.

CORRY: *(Standing)* There's no one left to ask. We're the last two on the train.

(They strap hang and sway about)

ANDY: I knew this would happen. It would have been so much easier by bus.

CORRY: What! Stuck in all that traffic! If we leap out at the next station we'll just about make it. Quickly, we need to be ready to get out. *(Pause) Now!*

(They stand ready facing the door)

ANDY: It's stopping. We must look for notices.

CORRY: Right. *Go!*

(They both leap forward)

by Kenneth Pickering

The Fossil Hunters

The scene takes place in the 1840s in an area along the English coast where fossils are being found. It is the time of the early Victorian fossil craze during which collectors would pay significant sums of money to obtain good and unusual specimens for their collections. ELIZA and JANE, whose fathers sell fossils, are searching where there has recently been a rock fall. They carry baskets and tools and are bare footed.

ELIZA: *(Carefully walking along the beach)* We must take great care Jane as we search along that undercut. *(Pointing)* It could be dangerous.

JANE: That storm last night has brought a goodly pile of rocks down.

ELIZA: All the better for fossil finding.

(JANE finds a rock pool and stands in it)

JANE: The sun has taken the chill off this pool. I love wriggling my toes in sea water…

ELIZA: Jane! We're here to look for fossils not play in rock pools.

JANE: I guess you're right. *(Reluctantly moving on)*

(They both start to look for fossils, bending down, picking up stones, tapping them with their tools and discarding the shards)

ELIZA: Look for the brown stones, they're the best. *(Picking one up)* This looks promising. One crack and look, a perfect leaf fossil. *(Showing the stone)*

JANE: Your Pa will get a good price for it when the collectors come. I've got to search harder. *(Bending down and picking up stones and tapping them)*

ELIZA: Let's look at those rocks that fell down last night. Over there. *(Pointing)* Come on…

(The two go over to where there are a pile of rocks, newly fallen from the rock face on the beach)

ELIZA: Look! That's a big brown lump. And it's got a crack in it...

JANE: It's a big 'un.

ELIZA: Right! You take that end and tap it, and I'll take this end and we'll see if it cracks open...

(They kneel down and start to hit the rock with their tools)

JANE: It's coming away!

ELIZA: Gentle now. Don't be too hard on it...

(The rock falls in two pieces revealing a large fossil)

JANE: Oh look! It's a whole sea creature...

ELIZA: One I've never seen the like of before...

JANE: It's a wonder.

ELIZA: A collector will pay our Pa's big money for this one.

(Suddenly, they see a group of boys approaching)

ELIZA: Quick, sit on it! Cover it up. Those Back Lane boys are coming over.

JANE: They'll take it from us...

ELIZA: Not if you sit on it so they can't see. Act fed up. Act tired. No! Better still, act sick, really sick. That'll get rid of them.

JANE: That big one frightens me. He's called Scrummer an' he's mean.

(The two try to hide the rock, JANE sitting on it and ELIZA kneeling)

ELIZA: *(Looking up at the boy)* No! We ain't found anything. We're resting before we go up to the village. Jane's feeling sick with a great pain in the stomach...

Continued ▸

JANE: *(Groaning)* It's getting worse. *(Starts to cry, then suddenly stops)* Did you hear that? It's a crack, like rocks cracking open. *(Pointing)* Up there, where the rocks fell down last night!

ELIZA: *(Jumping up)* We'll all get crushed...

JANE: I can't move for the pain! I'm frightened...

ELIZA: Don't leave us Scrummer... Stay and help...

(They watch as the boys run off)

JANE: *(Calling out)* Scrummer! Come back an' help me! *(They watch the boys go)*

ELIZA: Good, they've gone. You should go on the stage.

JANE: That's what my Ma says.

ELIZA: Right! You sit there and I'll get a wheelbarrow.

JANE: Sitting like a hen on her eggs.

ELIZA: Yes! But this fossil will get us a lot more money than eggs. *(Turning to leave)*

JANE: *(Calling out)* And bring straw to hide it under...

ELIZA: Think of the money Jane. Think of the money!

by Jeffrey Grenfell-Hill

Level 1 Acting

Grade 3 Solo

Titles in Level 1 Acting: Grade 3 Solo

Howl's Moving Castle

In the land of Ingary, where magical happenings are quite common, SOPHIE is the eldest of three sisters. She works in her late father's hat shop in the town of Market Chipping and talks to the hats as she trims them with ribbons and feathers, to make them attractive to sell. Sophie has no idea that a very dangerous customer is just about to enter the shop and change her life.

SOPHIE: *(Talking to the hat she is trimming)* You really are beautiful, you know… Red silk and a bunch of wax cherries. *(Putting it to one side, getting up and moving across the shop and picking up a plain black and white hat)* Now you are very stylish! I really like you.

(Putting the hat down and looking around her) But, look at the rest of you… watching me on stands or waiting to be trimmed. What good are you all? Did you know I lost a customer today? She stormed in whirling the pleated mushroom bonnet by its ribbons and complained that she had not met a Count… or anyone at all while she was wearing it! I said that I was not surprised and, with a face like hers, she wouldn't have had the wit to spot the King himself if he came begging! She threw the bonnet at me and stormed out of the shop!

(A very well dressed lady enters the shop)

Oh… another customer. What a grand one too, with a sable wrap, diamonds and a real ostrich plume in her hat! Well, she won't find anything here. None of these are in her class.

(She goes over to the lady and greets her) Would you like a hat madam? Can I help you choose one? As you see, we have a good selection. *(Fetching first one hat and then another)* Here's a very stylish black and white hat. … No? You don't like the pink one. What about this caterpillar green? *(Beginning to show her annoyance)* Well, we're only a small shop madam. You asked for hats. These are all we've got. I don't know why you bothered to come in.

Continued ▸

(The lady pulls back the feather that has been partly hiding her face and Sophie immediately jumps away from her, recognising who she is) Oh my goodness… I know who you are now! You're the Wicked Witch of the Waste. *(SOPHIE flinches as the Witch sprinkles a powder over her face)* AAAARGH! What was that? What have you thrown on me? *(Her voice starts to croak)* There must be some mistake. What are you staring at?

(The Witch sweeps out of the shop and Sophie puts her hands to her face)

(Even more croakily) Oh, what has happened to my face? My hands? They're covered in wrinkles… with veins on the back and knuckles like knots. *(Looking down at her feet)* My feet too… my legs… they look as if I'm 90 years old!

(SOPHIE hobbles slowly to peer at her image in a mirror on the wall) She's turned me into an old woman!

by Diana Wynne Jones, adapted by LAMDA

Black Beauty

GINGER is a worn-out chestnut mare, once proud and beautiful. She has been sold many times and now works pulling a shabby cab. One day, lined up with other cab horses outside a park, she notices a particularly beautiful black cab horse and is sure that she recognises her from happier times.

GINGER: Black Beauty, is that you?

It's me. Ginger! I've changed a lot. You might find it hard to recognise me now… But I'd know you anywhere.

(Beauty sidles up to be closer and looks at her)

It seems so long ago that we were together. Where have you been? I can see that you've been treated well. It took me a year before they considered that I was fit for work. I stayed at Earlshall before they sold me off to a gentleman. *(Wistfully)* That was wonderful. He was good to me.

I would run and canter and gallop… in acres of fresh green countryside. *(Looking around her and trying to suppress a cough)* How I miss that now! Life was good for a while… as it must have been good for you.

(She edges away from Beauty)

Things didn't work out though. One day, after a longer gallop than usual the old strain returned. I was no longer any use to the gentleman. He did look after me… got me medical help and allowed me to rest… but then he sold me. In this way I changed hands several times, but always getting lower down. No smart cabs for me!

(Looking around her and moving back towards Beauty, and suppressing another bout of coughing)

Continued ▸

You look well off, and I am glad of it, but I could not tell you what my life has been. When they found out my weakness they said I was not worth what they gave for me, and that I must go into one of the low cabs, and just be used up; that is what they are doing, whipping and working with never one thought of what I suffer – they paid for me, and must get it out of me, they say.

I used to stand up for myself if I was ever ill-used, but it's no use; men are strongest, and if they are cruel and have no feeling, there is nothing that we can do, but just bear it – bear it on and on to the end.

(Coughing again, and looking sadly at Beauty) I wish the end would come, I wish I was dead. I have seen dead horses, and I am sure they do not suffer pain; I wish I may drop down dead at my work, and not be sent off to the knackers.

You are the only friend I ever had.

Goodbye Beauty. Here comes my master.

(GINGER's driver comes up to lead her away. She jerks her head backwards and, with a newfound sense of pride, tosses her thin mane and painfully walks away. She stops and turns to have one last look at Beauty, but he tugs her mouth, and she walks off)

by Anna Sewell, adapted by LAMDA

In Portia's Kitchen

In the world of Shakespeare's The Merchant of Venice, *MARIO/MARIA, a kitchen boy or girl, is preparing food at a big kitchen table spread with utensils and vegetables. The house belongs to the heiress Portia, but she is away from home and her friends Lorenzo and Jessica are staying in the house. The servant is unhappy about this situation – and especially about Jessica's pet monkey.*

MARIO/MARIA: Ever since Lord Lorenzo came with his new wife Jessica this household has not been the same... *(Goes to the fireplace and pours a jug of water into a pot, then tosses in the vegetables)* She flounces up to the best guest chamber and says "her husband is now in charge" and she "will mistress the lot of us!" *(Returning to the table to continue chopping vegetables)* So what happens? One of those tinkers from down south turns up outside with his tray of ribbons an' such, playing a tune on his flute and with a dancing monkey at his heel... And what does she do? Rushes out... all excited... and begs the tinker to sell his monkey to her... Now he's not about to part with the creature easily as he sees his chance to get a good price... He hangs out saying "No! no!" to the coins she has in her pocket... And then she rushes back in here to her chamber and gets this casket... and off she runs after the tinker offering him a ring... when he sees it his nasty little tinker eyes light up and he takes the ring and hands over the monkey... Lady Jessica is as pleased as punch... But I'm not I can tell you...

What does she do with this monkey each morning? She ties the creature to the lemon tree that grows in our courtyard... and that rope tied around his waist is so long he can jump up at that window *(pointing)* ... and come in here...and what does that nasty little creature do? ... He sneers and laughs at me in a devilish way and tosses all my pots and pans around... And he makes a bee-line for the candied fruits and stuffs them in his mouth... Oh! I hate the little monster... What he does not eat he throws on the floor... You should have seen the place when he discovered where the eggs

Continued ▸

are kept… our Steward has asked Lady Jessica to shorten the rope, but she laughs and says "monkeys need to jump around"… Jump around! I'd like to jump on him! We can't wait for our Lady Portia to return… She will get things back to normal… Oh! There's that creature… *(The monkey appears at the window)* Don't you come in here you little devil… *(Getting a broom to frighten the monkey with)* … Get back into the yard… *(Brandishing the broom)* Go on! In the yard where you belong. *(Drops the broom and screams as the monkey jumps on to his/her shoulder)* Ah! Oh! Help! … Get off me! … get off you horrible creature *(Falling to the floor)* … Oh Lord! Save me… save me… *(Struggling with the monkey)*

by Jeffrey Grenfell-Hill

The Train

TIMOTHY is an eleven-year-old boy who never does as he is told. He is travelling with his mother, father and sister on a train bound for the south of France. It is a long, hot journey and he is becoming bored and restless. When the train pulls into a station he persuades his father to let him climb down on to the platform in search of an ice-cream. Other people have had the same idea and the station is crowded with people running and pushing in all directions.

TIMOTHY: *(Speaking to his father)* Come on Dad – we have only got a few minutes before we have to get back on the train again! I'm so hot and thirsty. Aren't you? Phew! I think it's even hotter on the platform than it was on the train and we're not even halfway yet! Let's find those ice-creams. You go over that side and I'll try here. *(Looking around him)* There are so many stalls – newspapers, magazines. *(Forgetting that his father is no longer next to him)* Dad. Dad. Look at this comic. It's Tintin! We read about him in school. *(Picking up the comic book)* But it's in French! I can't understand a word. *(At that moment a group of noisy children push past him, knocking the comic book out of his hand and almost knocking him to the ground)*. Hey, look where you're going. Now I've dropped my money! I've got to find it. Coins can roll anywhere. *(Scrambling down onto the floor and picking his way between legs on the crowded platform)* Sorry sir, I didn't mean to tread on you. Excuse me. *(Trying to make himself understood) Excusez-moi madame*, it's my money. I've dropped it!

(An elderly lady swipes him with her umbrella and he moves back very quickly) There's no need to hit me madame. I'm not trying to take your bag. I'm not after money. I want to find my own! *(Getting up and moving to the side, TIMOTHY suddenly notices a coin on the floor)* There it is! *(He swerves, weaves and pushes past people and picks his coin up)* That's my money! I didn't steal. I dropped it when I was pushed. *(The old lady has now caught up with TIMOTHY. She is still shaking her umbrella at him and is calling him a thief. A small crowd has begun to gather round him)*

Continued ▸

Oh I wish I was better at French. They just don't understand me. Please don't shake your umbrella at me again, madame! *(As TIMOTHY tries to explain to the group of onlookers what has happened, he mimes the actions to try and make them understand)* I was pushed by some children. They knocked the money out of my hand. *(Holding up the coin in desperation)* This is my money! Oh, what are you all staring at? All I wanted was an ice-cream. Ice-cream! Ice-cream! It doesn't matter anyway. *(Looking around him and beginning to panic)* I've lost my father now, too... Dad. Dad! *(Jumping up and down to gain attention)* I'm over here! *(Waving)* Here! *(Turning to the people around him)* You can't stop me from leaving. Take the money! I don't want one of your ice-creams anyway. It would make me sick! I hate it here... and I want my father.

(TIMOTHY suddenly hears the warning whistle of the departing train. He pushes free from the crowd and begins to run aimlessly, weaving his way through the crowd) The train! Oh no! It's going. Help! Stop it! I've got to get on. Mum... Dad... Susan. HELP! *(To himself)* Oh, it's no use. It's going! Stop the train! Please!

by Jacqueline Emery

The Wild Animal Song Contest

This play describes a competition to see which animal from which nation can produce the best song. Kingsley DEBIT, a King Penguin, is the show's compère. This scene takes place in the dressing room where Debit, with a fake handmike, is conducting a rehearsal.

DEBIT: We've got to get on with rehearsals. First of all, I'll remind you of the rules. Rule One: each animal shall perform a song written by itself. Rule Two: each animal will be interviewed before performing and reply politely when asked about its hobbies and ambitions. Rule Three: political songs – about famine, unemployment or peace – are not to be sung. Rule Four: there must be no songs which make fun of human beings or penguins. Rule Five: for the contest itself, but not for rehearsals, the singers will perform wearing human being costumes and masks. This will add dignity to the proceedings. Rule Six: the winner will be awarded the title, King or Queen of the Animals, and will be presented with the Million Gun plus one hundred thousand bullets for the Million Gun. It's the gun which kills a million animals with every bullet. It's the greatest gun, and it's the only one. Now, we've just time to rehearse the show. I'll take Quilla in front of the cameras first. The rest of you – vanish yourselves and get ready.

(DEBIT takes his handmike and steps into the screen)

I'm going to start the rehearsal now! Action! And now I'd like to introduce the unique, the amazing, the absolutely superfluous Inter-Galactic Universal Wild Animal Song Contest, coming to you live from… *(Insert name of venue)*

I'm your loveable compère, my name's Kingsley Debit, and we're going to have fun, fun, fun and win the Million Gun! And here comes our first competitor. Will you please put your wings together for Quilla, the Golden Eagle.

by Adrian Mitchell

Good Impressions

NATALIE's parents are divorced and she is about to meet her dad's new girlfriend for the very first time. She is nervous about this meeting as she wants to make a good impression but she is also worried that she won't like her. In this scene, Natalie is talking to one of her friends about the impending meeting.

NATALIE: You're not being any help at all. You're supposed to be here to help me decide what to wear and all you've done so far is sit there and flick through that stupid magazine. Don't you know that there are more important things in life? ... because I want to look my best... because I want her to like me... because it means a lot to my dad, that's why. I want to make a good impression. He must really like her because he's never introduced me to any of his girlfriends before. So it must be serious... He's just going out with her, of course he's not going to marry her... is he? ... But then she'll be my stepmother... I don't know that I want another mum, I mean I've got one already and I don't think I want to decide between two of them, it could get really confusing... don't be silly, not all stepmothers are evil, that's just in fairytales, they're not really true you know... Sammie's stepmum wasn't very nice to her because she kept running away – she had a right to get cross but Alice's stepmum is always really nice and she makes cakes, and takes her shopping... Maybe they just seem nice to start with to get 'the dad' and then they change into these horrible, evil people who trap you and do magic spells on you to get rid of you... I hadn't thought of that. Maybe they weren't fairytales after all. Maybe it's all actually true, the evil stepmother is a real person! Well then I don't want to make a good impression at all, in fact I'm going to make a really bad impression. I'm going to look dreadful. I'm not going to wear any make-up, I'll wear my baggy old jeans with holes and make my hair look all messy. I'll grunt and mumble and I won't answer when she talks to me, and I'll look at the floor and shuffle my feet. Then she won't like me, and she'll never marry my dad because she'll never want to go near me again... job done!

by Emma-Louise Tinniswood

Never Could Say Goodbye

A summer Sunday. Twelve-year-old HARRIET is helping her best friend Ayesha to clear out her grandfather's garden shed while he is out for the day playing golf.

HARRIET: Smells of damp wood in there. All those dried up pots of paint. He must be a busy man your Grandad. Old brushes, rusty nails, jam jars full of goodness knows what. What's it you call someone who saves things? A hoarder that's it, your Grandad's a hoarder. They say a lot of men get like that after a certain age. Can't bear to part with stuff, even when it's of no use to them or anyone else any more. When he comes home he won't know what's hit him. He won't be able to find anything; even when we've got it all organised. He'll complain, you watch, he'll prefer the clutter.

(HARRIET sits down on a homemade garden bench close to the shed)

My Grandpa's shed was the same… only more cobwebs. The spiders were everywhere. All shapes and sizes. He called his garden shed his special place. Never could say goodbye to anything. When we used to go and visit him and it was time to go home, he'd disappear. We'd kiss Gran goodbye and ask where Grandpa was and he'd have nipped to the shop or taken the dog for a walk. The last night at the hospital, when we all knew it was time to say goodbye, he whispered some excuse to see the nurse. We all had to wait outside. She came out and said he'd fallen asleep and that visiting time was over so we might as well go home. Well he died that night. He'd managed to avoid saying goodbye to the end. He'd been an evacuee in World War Two. Gran said he'd shouted goodbye to his mother from the train as she waved him off. He went to live in the countryside. Sent letters home of course and got letters back. That's how it was for all of them. Then he got told that he couldn't go back home because, well, there was no home to go to. My great Gran and Gramps adopted him. He didn't see his real

Continued ▸

parents again. Gran says that when he was grown up with his own family, he was a bit embarrassed about being abandoned and he'd always had this thing about saying goodbye – just couldn't bring himself to say it again… ever.

(HARRIET looks back at the shed, deep in thought)

You know Ayesha, I think we should put all your Grandad's stuff in some bin-liners, let him sort through them when he gets back…

by Nick Teed

A Maple Leaf Wonder

SUZIE is a keen TV Chef watcher. She has decided to make her own recipes while her mother is out. Her mother is very house-proud so Suzie is anxious not to ruin the kitchen.

SUZIE: Right, now where to start. *(Searches the cupboards)* Ah – sugar, flour, eggs... *(Checks)* Oh well, four will have to do... *(Selects ingredients)* Bread, one can of peaches, nutmeg... Now we need a bowl and a baking tray, not forgetting the apron. *(She puts apron on and is immediately transformed into a TV Chef)*

Hello viewers. I've brought all these ingredients to show you how to make a... *(Pauses to think of a name)* ... Maple-Leaf Wonder. Firstly you take a handful of sugar and flour. Place them in the bowl and add four eggs. *(Finding it difficult to get a handful of flour, she pours it into the bowl)* I've watched my mother doing this. *(There is a cloud of flour which makes her cough)* Break the eggs into the mixture. *(Does so)* And mix using your fingertips. *(Mixing slowly)* It does tend to stick a bit but you can always lick it off. Now add the peaches. Oh, I need a can opener and my hands are a bit messy. *(Gets mixture all over worktop and can opener which won't grip the can)*

Now with your hands mix in the peaches. It's a bit sloppy but remember, this is fun, fun, *(grimaces while mixing)* fun. Now for the nutmeg. *(She considers and pours a little, then she pours all the nutmeg into the bowl)* We mustn't forget the bread, which of course I would have prepared earlier. *(With messy hands places the sliced bread round the baking tray)* And this should have been greased. *(Getting flustered)* Oh well, forget the greasing – and pour on... or lump on the peach mixture. *(Does so)* There. *(Relieved)* And bake it in a pre-heated oven, which I forgot to turn on, for 20 minutes. So, let's make that 30 minutes.

Continued ▸

(Moves the dial on the cooker. She suddenly hears something just as she's putting the mixture in the oven. She throws off her apron, uses it to wipe the work-top and her hands and turns her back to the oven door as if to hide it. She calls) Mum! Is that you?… You're early. I've got a surprise for you. *(Licking her fingers)*... I'll tidy the kitchen later…

No, it's not too bad. *(Looks around the kitchen)* Really.

by Clare Price

The Phoenix and the Carpet

Robert, Anthea, Cyril, Jane and their baby brother the Lamb are desperate to liven up a boring afternoon. They have drawn magical symbols in chalk near the fireplace and burned some aromatic wood. On the mantelpiece is a mysterious egg which has recently arrived in the house. Robert accidentally knocks the egg off the mantelpiece into the fire. The egg cracks open, and from within the fire emerges the PHOENIX, a gold-feathered creature the size of a chicken.

PHOENIX: Which of you put the egg into the fire?

(The bird looks around, then bows in a bird-like manner to Robert)

I am your grateful debtor. Do you know who I am? I am the Phoenix. My fame has lived for two thousand years. Allow me to look at my portrait.

(The Phoenix cocks its head to one side)

It's not a flattering likeness. Phoenix – in ornithology – is a fabulous bird of antiquity. *Antiquity* is quite correct. But fabulous? Well, do I look it? At least I *am* the only one of my kind.

(The Phoenix whirrs his golden wings and flutters to the table)

I'm nearly cool now. *(Turning to Robert)* I will not vanish or anything sudden. *(To all the children)* I will tell you my tale. I had resided for many thousand years in the wilderness, and I was becoming weary of the monotony of my existence. But I acquired the habit of laying my egg and burning myself every five hundred years – and you know how difficult it is to break yourself of a habit.

I awoke one morning from a feverish dream and I saw two people, a man and a woman. They were a prince and princess, and the story of their parents was one which I am sure you will like to hear. In early youth the mother of the princess happened to hear the story of a

Continued ▸

certain enchanter… well, to cut about seventy long stories short, this prince and princess were so fond of each other that they did not want anyone else, and the enchanter had given them a magic carpet (you've heard of a magic carpet?) and they had just sat on it and told it to take them right away from everyone – and it had brought them to the wilderness. And as they had no further use for the carpet, they gave it to me. That was indeed the chance of a lifetime!

Well, I got the prince to lay out the carpet, and I laid my egg on it; then I said, "Now, my excellent carpet, prove your worth. Take that egg somewhere where it can't be hatched for two thousand years, and where, when that time's up, someone will light a fire of sweet wood and aromatic gums, and put the egg in to hatch." And you see, it's all come out exactly as I said. The words were no sooner out of my beak than egg and carpet disappeared. I burnt myself up and knew no more till I awoke over there. *(Pointing to the fire)*

(There is the sound of a key turning in the lock, and the Phoenix pauses)

Oh, here's your father! You should all be in bed, so wish yourselves there, and wish the carpet back in its place. *(Whispering)* I shall sleep on the cornice above your curtains. Please don't tell anyone about me.

by E Nesbit, adapted by LAMDA

The Brothers Lionheart

Two brothers, RUSKY and Jonathan, have been reunited in Nangiyala, a land of legend and adventure. But Rusky's older brother Jonathan has now left him at their home, Knights Farm, to go and face a fearful enemy alone. Rusky fears for his brother's safety and wonders what he should do.

RUSKY: It felt cold as I crept into my bed, but I soon fell asleep. And I dreamt about Jonathan. The dream was so terrifying that it woke me up. "Yes, Jonathan!" I cried. "I'm coming!" And I rushed out of bed. In the darkness around me, there seemed to be echoes of wild cries. Jonathan's cries! He had called to me in my dream that he needed help. I knew it. I could still hear him, and I wanted to rush straight out into the dark night to get to him, wherever he was. But I realised how impossible that was.

What could I do? No one was as helpless as I was! I could only creep back into my bed again and lie there trembling, feeling lost and small and afraid and lonely, the loneliest person in the whole world, I thought.

The next morning, I sat for hours out with my rabbits and thought about what I should do. I had no one to talk to, no one to ask. My brother had called for me, so didn't I have to go out and try to find him? I had to decide for myself. I couldn't go to Sofia, because she would stop me. She would never let me go. She was not that foolish. It was foolish, I'm sure, what I wanted to do. And dangerous, too. The most dangerous thing of all. And I wasn't at all brave.

Continued ▸

I don't know how long I sat there, leaning against the stable wall, tearing up grass. I tore off every blade of grass around about me, but I didn't notice until afterwards, not while I'd been sitting there being tormented. The hours went by. Perhaps I would be sitting there still, if I hadn't suddenly remembered what Jonathan had said. That sometimes you have to do things that are dangerous. Otherwise you weren't a human being, but a bit of filth.

So I decided. I banged my fist down on the rabbit hutch so that the rabbits jumped and I said out loud so that it should be certain: "I'll do it! I'll do it! I'm not a bit of filth."

by Astrid Lindgren, translated by Joan Tate and adapted by LAMDA

Level 1 Acting

Grade 3 Duologue

Titles in Level 1 Acting: Grade 3 Duologue

Dolphin Summer

RISSA and TAMZIN are best friends who live on Romney Marsh in Sussex, on the south coast of England. While Rissa is practical and Tamzin is dreamy, they are united by a very long friendship, their love of ponies and their passion for everything to do with their coastal home. In this scene, they have gone riding by moonlight on the beach. Tamzin is looking for dolphins.

(RISSA and TAMZIN have dismounted from their ponies on the beach)

RISSA: We have all the Marsh to ourselves.

TAMZIN: Except for the sheep. I do wish they wouldn't go to sleep in the middle of the path and then leap up so frantically.

RISSA: You've got nothing to complain of. Cascade is such a well-behaved pony. Everything sends Siani into a panic.

TAMZIN: The only net-shed that has two good hooks on the wall, for tying the ponies, is the farthest one away towards the river. I think they used them for drying nets when they went fishing off the shore.

(They tie the ponies to the shed)

RISSA: Now the wind's dropped it's warm enough to undress on the beach, though the shed is open. There's nobody for miles.

TAMZIN: *(Peering out to sea)* I keep thinking I can see dolphins out there.

RISSA: I think it's only waves. The way they look in the moonlight.

TAMZIN: The ponies are staring out, too. I was imagining Cascade was a sea-horse. Perhaps he's longing to get back. But I don't think we'd see any dolphins if we went in on the ponies.

Continued ▸

RISSA: The tide could be higher, but never mind. Are you ready?

TAMZIN: Ouch! The stones are painful here. My feet are never really hard until the summer holidays.

RISSA: You know, it could be either waves or dolphins out there.

(They enter the water)

TAMZIN: Perhaps if we swim out farther we'll see if there are really dolphins. The water is warm!

RISSA: It always is when the air is cold; it's the contrast.

TAMZIN: I could go on and on… right to France.

RISSA: We've come out quite a way, already. Never mind about the dolphins… The stars are amazing, look. I know the Great Bear, anyway. And that's the Pleiades… I hope the ponies are all right.

(TAMZIN gets caught in an undertow and disappears from view. RISSA is unaware of this and continues talking)

It is so beautiful here. I could stay here forever, couldn't you? *(Pause)* Tamzin… you're not listening. *(Looking around)* Tamzin. Tamzin! *(Horrified, turning in circles in the water, looking around)* Where are you? *(To herself)* Where is she? She can't have hidden underwater for this long. Oh no… no… She might have drowned. What should I do? *(She wades back to the water's edge and looks all around her)* I just don't know what to do… I suppose I should get help… but then again, I ought to try and find her.

(Meanwhile, TAMZIN has crawled back onto the beach)

TAMZIN: *(Weakly)* It's all right, Rissa. I'm over here.

RISSA: *(Running over to TAMZIN and crouching beside her)* Tamzin! What happened? Where did you go? You're all right, now! I'll look after you. Everything will be all right. Wait… I'm just going to get clothes and towels. I won't be a minute. *(Runs up the beach and returns a moment later, wraps a towel around TAMZIN)* I'm so glad you're all right. I'll look after you.

TAMZIN: Thanks.

RISSA: Are you warmer? Do you feel better?

TAMZIN: Yes… yes. *(Pause)* I got caught in an undertow, I think. I found myself being sucked down... I couldn't keep my head above the water. I was so scared…

RISSA: But how did you break free?

TAMZIN: I was sinking down – and down. Then suddenly something pushed me upwards – and I could breathe again. It kept on pushing – then I realised – it was a dolphin! Then another dolphin came along and they pushed me back to shore. Just like Arion.

RISSA: Like what?

TAMZIN: Someone in a story.

RISSA: Could you get on Cascade? With me helping.

TAMZIN: I think so. I'm all right. Just a bit wobbly.

RISSA: Just lean on me while we walk up there. *(They walk slowly up the beach)* I can't believe that the dolphins actually saved you. *(Hesitates)* I thought you were dead.

TAMZIN: I thought I was going to be.

by Monica Edwards, adapted by LAMDA

Stowaways

The year is 1912. EMMA is the orphaned daughter of a country vicar. She has been living in Liverpool with her aunt Millicent and cousin Arthur. They have been treating her like a servant, however, and she can't wait to escape from them and begin a new life on her own. LILY is the daughter of Maggie May, a music hall singer and dancer. She is constantly on tour but has recently been living in Blackpool with Nathan, a dashing American vaudeville performer, with whom she has become infatuated. She no longer has time to spend with her daughter. Lily has heard Nathan speak about his home country with such a sense of wonder and excitement that she has decided to see it for herself.

The scene takes place in the hold of an ocean liner. It is crowded with boxes, trunks and cases. Emma and Lily have both decided to stow away on the ship and have crept in separately to hide. Neither knows that the other girl is there.

EMMA: *(Slowly climbing out from behind a pile of trunks and packing cases)* What an amazing place! *(Looking around her)* This is so vast. – It's like a cathedral. If I stand very still I can almost feel the sea. *(The ship lurches a little and EMMA nearly loses her balance)* Whoops! We must have got into the open water by now. America, here we come! I think it's safe to come out. Even if they find me, it's too late to send me back. I could always work my passage. I could... *(A loud noise interrupts her)*

LILY: *(From inside one of the large trunks)* Oooooowwwwwww!!!

EMMA: *(Looking around her)* What was that?

LILY: *(Louder)* Oooooowwwwwww!!!

EMMA: *(Going back into hiding)* There's someone else in here. I'm not alone! Who is it? What shall I do?

LILY: *(Pushing up the lid of the trunk and sitting upright)* Ooh – that's better. I had cramp. It's really painful. It was also quite spooky with the lid shut! Like being inside a coffin. Poor old 'Magic Bones'.

When he comes to do his act, he'll find that half his costumes are no longer in his trunk!!! Shame I had to throw them out. There just wasn't enough room for me as well. *(Climbing carefully out of the trunk)* Hello, by the way. I know you're there. *(Waiting for a reply)* Don't be scared. You can show yourself to me.

EMMA: *(Slowly emerging from her hiding place)* Hello.

LILY: So you're a stowaway too? *(Going towards EMMA and helping her up)* I'm Lily.

EMMA: Emma... Emma Browning. I'm going to start a new life in America.

LILY: Just like me! *(Looking around her)* This is an amazing ship. So smart and fashionable. They even say it can't sink.

EMMA: It's enormous. There are so many decks. Do you think we can remain hidden?

LILY: We'll have to try and steal food... but, there are two of us now, so that will be easier. One of us can keep watch, or distract people.

EMMA: While the other one takes the food!

LILY: Anyway, there must be so much waste on a ship like this. Rich people getting greedy!

EMMA: I thought trays with left-over food would be put in the corridors outside the first class staterooms. They do that in hotels. My father told me.

LILY: This is a ship, silly! The trays would just roll all over the place. *(Laughing)* You haven't travelled much, have you?

EMMA: *(Sitting on a trunk)* No. I lived in a small village with my father. He was the vicar. My mother died when I was born. My father was a kind and gentle man. He always cared for people. He caught the influenza visiting a sick parishioner. *(Sadly)* I never saw him again. He died the next night.

Continued ▸

LILY: And you ran away then?

EMMA: No. My aunt took me in. My mother's sister. She was so cold and distant, and my cousin Arthur treated me like a servant. "Fetch this," "Do that," "Make this," "Sweep that!" Then, I saw an advertisement about this ship.

LILY: So did I! I'm an actress. I could become famous in New York.

EMMA: *(Standing up and looking at her with admiration)* An actress! A real actress! You mean... you've been in plays... on the stage? *(Looking at her closely)* But, how can this be true? You're my age. Just a child!

LILY: *(Dancing around the packing cases)* Actress... Dancer... Singer... I can do them all! My mother can and Nathan, her gentleman friend, said that I could be just like her one day. *(The ship lurches again and she falls on the floor)* Whoops! How do they manage to put on shows when the ship is at sea?

EMMA: I wonder what New York is like?

LILY: Nathan told me. He was born in America. He said the streets of New York are paved with gold and that anyone can do well if they work hard. There are theatres everywhere.

EMMA: And lots of people from all over the world. Just like us... looking for a new life.

LILY: Excitement!

EMMA: New beginnings!

LILY: When my mother and Nathan celebrate, they always have a drink.

EMMA: We could pretend. What shall we drink to?

LILY: To our future!

EMMA: Our future!

LILY: To America!

EMMA: America!

LILY: To this ship!

EMMA AND LILY: *(Together)* The *Titanic*!

(The ship lurches again and both EMMA and LILY fall in a heap on the floor, laughing)

by Jacqueline Emery

Come On!

WIL and GEORGE are on an outdoor expedition and have come to a river which they must cross. The only means of crossing is by balancing on a tree which has fallen across the river. Wil is more confident than George.

(The imaginary tree trunk runs across the stage from left to right and GEORGE and WIL are standing on the bank of the river)

WIL: We've got to cross this river somehow. *(Catching sight of the fallen tree)* So we'll use this tree trunk. *(Feeling the trunk with a foot)* I think it's strong enough.

GEORGE: I'm not going over there. For a start, it's a very long way down if we fall!

WIL: *(Reassuringly)* We won't fall. It's quite wide.

GEORGE: It looks very slippery.

WIL: Why do you always think of problems? Just look on the bright side. We'll get across.

GEORGE: Well, you go first and then I'll follow. It's far too narrow for both of us to cross at the same time.

WIL: Alright. Here goes. *(WIL steps on to the tree trunk.)* I'll take it very slowly and be careful not to look down. *(Balancing)* I'm going to fix my eyes on that tree over there.

(WIL advances slowly with arms held out at the side and head up high)

GEORGE: You look like a tightrope walker.

WIL: I feel like one. You know, like those people who used to walk between two skyscrapers in New York!

GEORGE: I wish I was that confident. You're nearly there.

WIL: All you have to do is put one foot in front of the other and you'll get there easily. *(Stepping off the trunk onto the bank) Done it!* Ok, it's your turn.

(From this point onwards they call across the river to each other. GEORGE is growing very nervous and moves with great difficulty)

GEORGE: I don't like the look of this at all!

WIL: Come on now, just take your time. Put one foot on the trunk and you'll feel how firm it is.

GEORGE: I don't like looking ahead. I think I'll move sideways. I can balance better. *(Painfully turning sideways, swaying more and more and struggling to balance)*

WIL: Are you sure that's a good idea?

GEORGE: *(Wobbling about)* Aaaaaa… ggh… this is horrible! I can feel myself swaying all over the place.

WIL: Come on. Move your left foot. No, more than that!

GEORGE: *(Too terrified to move)* I can't! … my foot is stuck. It won't move.

WIL: Yes it will. Just put all your weight on your right foot for a moment and then move your left.

GEORGE: I can't think which foot is which, you're confusing me.

WIL: *(Getting very irritated)* You're hopeless. *(Trying to be patient)* Look! gradually edge your foot around until you're facing me. Come on, you can do it.

(GEORGE gradually manages to accomplish this)

GEORGE: Ooo… eer.

WIL: Right! Now hold your arms out to the side. That's it. *(Pause)* Now come towards me. That's it! *(Pause)* Slowly, slowly. You're getting there.

Continued ▸

GEORGE: Oh! I wish the wind would stop blowing.

WIL: Don't worry about the wind. It's not that bad. Are you ok?

GEORGE: *(Quietly through gritted teeth)* Yes.

WIL: I can't hear you.

GEORGE: *(Through teeth)* Yeeeesss.

WIL: Why are you talking in that strange way? Open your mouth.

GEORGE: I can't! My teeth are stuck together.

WIL: You're nearly there. That's it. Come on... *(Reaching out a hand)* take hold of my hand... one more step. That's it! Well done! You've made it!

GEORGE: *(Collapsing with relief)* Phew! That was terrible! I was terrified. I'm finished. I haven't an ounce of energy left.

WIL: Let's have a bar of chocolate.

GEORGE: Good idea! Where is it?

WIL: In your rucksack.

GEORGE: In my... *(Suddenly realising that the rucksack has been left on the other bank)* ... I don't believe it! *(Looking helplessly at the rucksack in the distance)* I... I left it behind.

(They remain still and glare at each other)

by Kenneth Pickering

The Merlin Conspiracy

This is a story about parallel worlds. In the land of Blest, two children in the Royal Court named Roddy and Grundo believe that the death of the 'Merlin' – the land's magical governor – was not natural. They enlist the help of NICK Mallory, a boy from another world – our world – to help them discover the truth. Nick encounters some strange people in his quest. In this scene, he is looking for the wizard Romanov and meets the elephant MINI.

(NICK enters trying to decide which path to take)

NICK: How am I going to know if a path I need goes off to the right? Perhaps if I get myself to the middle and sort of grope along there with one hand out in front. Aaargh! What's that? Something dabbed at me, something wet and cold and desperate. It groped my hand and then my face. *(NICK screams, steps backwards and sits down in a puddle)* I'm sure it's a snake. I don't like snakes.

MINI: *(Shrieking and falling backwards too)* Oh, *please*! *Help* me! I'm lost! I'm *stuck*!

NICK: What kind of snake are you?

MINI: I'm *not* a snake! I'm an elephant!

NICK: Elephants that talk! But I've already met a panther that I could understand, so why not? It all seems like one long, mad dream.

MINI: It's more like a nightmare, *I* think. And I'm not exactly talking. You must be good at picking up four-legged thoughts. *Please* help me!

NICK: OK, OK. I'm supposed to help you anyway. Where do you want to go?

MINI: Not *this* way! It's all so dark and I can't turn *round*! *(Squealing and trampling in panic)*

Continued ▸

NICK: *Stop it!* Shut up this moment or I won't help you!

MINI: *(Shuts up almost at once)* Sorry.

NICK: That's better. Getting in a panic in this place just makes it worse. Where are you from? How did you get here?

MINI: I was in the circus, outside the big top, waiting for my turn to go on, when all of a sudden there was this great whirling wind. All the tents came down or blew away, and people were screaming. I'm afraid I screamed too and ran away. I found a path that looked safe and I ran and ran, until it all got too narrow and...

NICK: Steady, steady! What did they call you in your circus?

MINI: Mini.

NICK: Mini! An elephant called Mini!

MINI: Short for Pudmini. I'm a *lady* elephant.

NICK: And I'm a gentleman human, and how I got here is a long story. My name is Nick – short for Nichothodes, if you want to know – and I'm on my way to see someone called Romanov. He'll be able to help both of us. So, if you just let me help you turn around...

MINI: I *can't* turn around! It's not *wide* enough!

NICK: Yes, it is. Or I can guide you backwards...

MINI: I'm not *good* at going backwards!

NICK: Then we'll go forwards, very steadily and carefully. *(Reaching up, finding her waving trunk and grabbing it)* Now come along. Forward carefully. Now stop... to the right... No! No! I mean left... yes... that's better. Wait! Stop!

MINI: I can't see anything! It's dark! Ouch! You're hurting my trunk! Nooo, that's my tusk!

NICK: Sorry! Is that better?

MINI: I've still got my harness on. Why don't you take hold of that?

(NICK feels about again and finds jingly leather somewhere on her face. He takes hold of it and pulls her confidently sideways)

MINI: I'm stuck! I'm stuck sideways now. *(Trumpeting)* Ooooh! Oooh! Ooh!

NICK: Stop it, stop it, stop it! Or I'll go away and leave you here! Calm *down!*

MINI: Oh, I can't, I *can't*!

NICK: Stand still! Where's the back of you?

MINI: Jammed right up against the cliff. I want to *kick*!

NICK: Well, don't. It won't help. What you need to do now is walk your front feet up the cliff this side until you're reared up, and then walk your back feet forward away from the cliff behind you. After that, you walk your *front* feet round to the left, so you come down facing the other way. Can you do that?

MINI: I don't *know*!

NICK: You can. You've been trained to stand on your hind legs. That will help. Now – let's try!

by Diana Wynne Jones, adapted by LAMDA

The Final Snore

CHRIS and OLIVER are away on a school adventure course for a week in the school holidays. They are meant to be asleep in a dormitory of boys. It is night time. They are in a bunk bed. Oliver is on the top bunk and Chris is underneath.

OLIVER: *(In a voiced whisper)* Psst! Chris. Can you hear me? *(He gets his torch and shines it on CHRIS)*

(CHRIS wakes with a start looking up to see OLIVER)

CHRIS: I wish you wouldn't keep doing that.

OLIVER: Sh! You'll wake the others.

CHRIS: *(Voiced whisper)* What time is it? I must get some sleep. I'm in the athletics team tomorrow morning.

OLIVER: It's that noise again. I can't sleep.

CHRIS: I could sleep if I was allowed to. We're only here until the weekend. Can't you just suffer it till then?

OLIVER: *(Climbing down from bunk bed, shines torch and walks towards doorway)* There's a faint tapping noise, like last night and the night before. It's probably someone trying to scare us.

CHRIS: *(Unconvinced)* Probably a dripping tap.

OLIVER: That's what you said last night. Anyway, we checked the shower block then. No, I think it's coming from the hall.

CHRIS: *(Getting out of bed. Slips dressing gown on)* I suppose there'll be no peace until we find out.

(OLIVER opens the door slowly, checking to see if there's any teacher around)

OLIVER: Come on.

CHRIS: *(Slips trainers on)* Hang on. This time I'm going to be prepared. I was frozen after last night's midnight search.

(They exit the dormitory and walk stealthily through the corridor, briefly making gestures outside a teacher's door)

OLIVER: He's got a loud snore.

CHRIS: Is that the noise that kept you awake?

OLIVER: No, that's a bigger drip.

(Both giggle. They reach a big door and enter into the great hall. Turning off their torch and switching on main lights)

The noise is quite loud in here. It sounds as if it's coming from over there. *(Pointing. Moving closer)*

CHRIS: *(Slightly nervous. Looking at watch)* We'd better hurry. Mr Wieland does night rounds of the dorms at 12, and I don't like this. Let's go back.

OLIVER: *(Kneeling down, listening intently. Then lying down with his head on the floor)* I can hear it better here. It's coming from under the floor.

CHRIS: Please Oliver, let's go.

OLIVER: *(Sitting up, and while brushing the floor with his hand feels a lever)* This looks like a handle. *(Looking at CHRIS in excitement)* It might be a trap door. Give me a hand.

CHRIS: Oliver, please can we go now?

OLIVER: Just a quick look. We can't go back to the dorm without resolving this mystery, can we?

CHRIS: You mean you can't.

OLIVER: *(Trying to prise the trap door open)* Come on! It's stuck. I need help.

(CHRIS lends a hand and between them they eventually open it)

Continued ▸

OLIVER: *(Looking inside)* It's a well.

CHRIS: Smells damp.

OLIVER: Lend me one of your trainers.

CHRIS: Then can we go back? *(Taking off one trainer and handing it to OLIVER)* Why do you want it anyway?

(OLIVER throws it into the well)

Hey!

OLIVER: It's deep.

CHRIS: I don't care if it's in Australia. What about my shoe?

OLIVER: Relax. *(Leaning over in fascination)*

CHRIS: Tell me, how am I going to do Athletics tomorrow with only one trainer?

OLIVER: *(Ignoring)* 100 metres I'd say.

CHRIS: Or 100 metre race.

OLIVER: No, it's 100 metres deep.

CHRIS: *(Becoming annoyed. Raising voice)* This is the very last time you get me out of bed on some wild goose chase.

OLIVER: *(Hearing something. Getting up)* Now you've done it. Wieland's on the prowl.

CHRIS: *(Panicking)* Quickly, shut the hatch! I'll do the light. *(Noticing Mr Wieland opening the door to the hall)* He's coming in!

OLIVER: Don't worry. I have a plan. I thought this might happen. Do what I do.

(Mr Wieland enters the hall and OLIVER mimes sleepwalking back to where they came in, loudly snoring as he goes. CHRIS follows, head bowed, appearing embarrassed, as they approach the hall door where Mr Wieland is standing)

CHRIS: Sorry Sir.

by Clare Price

Below Stairs

This scene takes place below stairs in a grand Victorian house. The new maid LILY has been given the job of cleaning the cutlery. She is taking great care with each piece. Another maid, ALICE, bustles in. She has been at the house for a year and is very confident.

ALICE: How are you getting on? I hope you haven't left any smears. Mr Keeling will be furious if there are smears. We don't want that. His face goes a very funny colour when he's cross.

LILY: I've been ever so careful, Alice. Look.

(She hands her the fork she is working on. ALICE examines it)

ALICE: Not bad at all, Lily.

LILY: I got the cloth right down between the prongs.

ALICE: Tines.

LILY: I beg your pardon?

ALICE: They're called 'tines' not 'prongs'.

LILY: Really? What a funny word. You know a lot of things, don't you, Alice?

ALICE: I suppose I do. Now, you get on. I'll take the ones you've finished.

(She picks up a few pieces of cutlery)

Where are the others?

LILY: What others? They're all there.

ALICE: Is this all you've done? You've been at it for nearly an hour.

LILY: You told me to be careful.

ALICE: And you have been, I see that – but you have to be quick as well. The Prince is coming to dinner tomorrow, not next week. Honestly!

LILY: I'm sorry.

ALICE: It's no good being sorry, my girl. You'd better look lively. Come along, get a move on.

LILY: I'm doing my best.

ALICE: Don't answer me back, thank you very much.

LILY: But… I didn't mean…

ALICE: I'm your superior, you must obey me without question. It's no good looking so miserable. It's the same for all of us. You answer to me, I answer to Mrs Blandish, she answers to Mr Keeling. And he answers to the Master.

LILY: Oh Alice, I do understand. But I've tried so hard.

(LILY suddenly bursts into tears)

ALICE: For goodness' sake. We've no time for tears.

LILY: And I'm so tired.

ALICE: Of course you are. We all are when we start off. What did you expect?

LILY: I don't know. None of my family have been in service so nobody told me what it would be like. I thought it would be different.

ALICE: I suppose all you thought about was living in a beautiful house and seeing grand people doing marvellous things.

LILY: I knew I'd be working hard but, yes, I suppose I did. But I never see the Family at all – or if I do, it's by mistake and I have to turn my face to the wall until they've gone past.

ALICE: It's the same for all of us.

LILY: And now… Oh Alice, I never dreamed there were so many knives and forks in the whole world. And I have to polish every one.

Continued ▸

(ALICE takes pity on her)

ALICE: Pass me that spare cloth. I'll give you a hand.

LILY: Aren't you supposed to be doing something else?

ALICE: Yes, a dozen things. But I'll show you how it's done and then you'll know. Watch.

(She takes a fork and with three or four deft strokes of the duster, cleans it)

Like this. And this. And then this. *(Holding it up to the light)* Then you check it for smears and – hey presto! – on to the next one.

LILY: That's marvellous. I'll never do it as fast as that.

ALICE: You will, with a little practice. You'll find it becomes second nature. In a year or two, you'll be showing the next under-house-parlour-maid the tricks of the trade just as I'm showing you. You're a bright girl, Lily. Mrs Blandish is very pleased with your progress – though don't ever say I said so.

LILY: That's a relief. I keep thinking I'll be dismissed.

ALICE: No chance of that. Certainly not before the Prince comes to dinner, it's all hands to the pump till then.

(Companionably, they clean the cutlery together)

LILY: Have you ever seen the Prince?

ALICE: Once. Last year. He's a great friend of the Master, you know. All the staff lined up to greet him as he got out of his carriage.

LILY: Was he very handsome? I think he must be. Being a Prince.

ALICE: He's a grumpy old man with a white beard and a belly out to here.

LILY: But he's a Prince.

ALICE: *(Laughing)* Oh Lily, you do have a lot to learn. Now, let's stop talking and do these spoons.

LILY: Yes, Alice.

(They polish the spoons)

by Shaun McKenna

The Ice Dragon

JANE and GEORGE are letting off fireworks on the 11th of December to celebrate after the heir to the throne cuts his first tooth. All of their relatives have head colds, so the children are allowed to go out into the garden alone for the fireworks. Little do they know that their adventures that night will lead them to the Arctic regions and a great ice dragon.

JANE: It's so cold.

GEORGE: Is that why you're wearing your fur cape, and your thick gloves, and your hood with the silver fox fur on it made out of Mother's old muff?

JANE: *You're* wearing your overcoat with the three capes, and your blanket, and Father's sealskin travelling cap with the pieces that come down over your ears.

GEORGE: I've never been so cold in our own garden before. But it's worth it, to see all the fireworks.

JANE: Let's light our own firework.

(They light the firework, which fizzes a bit and soon goes out)

GEORGE: That was a rotten firework. Let's get up on the fence so that we can see the ones from next door. And the fireworks at the Crystal Palace are even better.

(They climb up on the fence)

JANE: Look... look, can you see that over there? Far away, at the edge of the dark world.

GEORGE: The row of lights?

JANE: Oh, how pretty! I wonder what they are. It looks as if the fairies were planting little shining baby trees and watering them with liquid light.

GEORGE: That's nonsense. It's the Aurora Borealis. You know, the Northern Lights. I learned about them at school.

JANE: But what is the Rory Bory what's-it's-name? Who lights it? What's it there for?

GEORGE: Well... I don't really know. But it has something to do with the Great Bear, and the Dipper, and the Plough.

JANE: And what are they?

GEORGE: Oh, they're the names of some of the star families.

JANE: I wish we could see those lights nearer. I wonder if the star families are nice families – the kind that Mother would like us to go to tea with, if we were little stars?

GEORGE: They aren't that sort of families at all, silly. I only said 'families' because a kid like you wouldn't have understood if I'd said constell-... constell-... Anyway, I've forgotten the end of the word. And the stars are all up in the sky, so you can't go to tea with them.

JANE: No, I know. I said if we were little stars.

GEORGE: But we aren't.

JANE: *(Sighing)* No. I know that. I'm not as stupid as you think, George. But the Tory Bories are somewhere at the edge. Couldn't we go and see them?

GEORGE: For someone your age, you don't have much sense. It's half the world away.

JANE: It looks very near.

GEORGE: They're close to the North Pole. Look here, I don't care about the Aurora Borealis, but I shouldn't mind discovering the North Pole. It's awfully difficult and dangerous, and then you come home and write a book about it with a lot of pictures, and everybody says how brave you are.

Continued ▸

JANE: *(Getting off the fence)* Oh George, let's! We shall never have such a chance again. All the grown-ups are indoors with colds. It would be so exciting. All alone by ourselves, and quite late, too.

GEORGE: *(Gloomily)* I'd go right enough if it wasn't for you. But you know they always say I lead you into mischief. And if we went to the North Pole I'm sure we should get our boots wet. And you remember what they said about not going on the grass.

JANE: They said the lawn. We're not going on the lawn. Oh George, let's! It doesn't look so very far. We could be back before they had time to get dreadfully angry.

GEORGE: All right. But remember, I don't want to go.

by E Nesbit, adapted by LAMDA

The Children of the New Forest

The story begins in 1647 during the period of Civil War in England. The Beverley family, Cavaliers and Royalists, have been orphaned. The Roundheads have attacked and burned their family mansion, Arnwood. The children have been rescued by a local gamekeeper, who has hidden them in his small cottage in the depths of the New Forest. His intention is to pass them off as his own family. In this scene, the gamekeeper's son JACOB is going to the cottage to keep the oldest child, EDWARD, informed about what has been happening at Arnwood. As he approaches the cottage Smoker, a large dog, growls till Jacob speaks to him, and Edward opens the door.

JACOB: Hush Smoker. Stop growling. *(Looking around)* At least I was not followed here. The undergrowth is so dense. No one could find the way. *(Knocking on the door of the cottage)* Edward! Edward! Come, open the door. Do not be afraid, it's only me.

EDWARD: *(Opening the door)* My sisters are in bed and fast asleep, Jacob, and Humphrey has been nodding this half hour. Had he not better go to bed before we go back?

JACOB: Going back is no longer an option. Come out, Master Edward and look. *(He takes EDWARD's arm and points towards the mansion, burning in the distance)*

EDWARD: Our house! It's burning! Those wicked men have set it alight. I didn't really believe that they would. I can see the glow between the trees, and the flames are rising higher and higher.

JACOB: I told you that it would be so. If you had stayed behind you would all have been burned in your beds, for they did not enter the house to see who was in it, but fired it as soon as they had surrounded it.

Continued ▸

EDWARD: And my aunt! Did she escape? Oh Jacob, don't hide anything from me – even if it is bad news.

JACOB: Your aunt is safe, Master Edward, and by this time at Lymington.

EDWARD: We will go to her tomorrow.

JACOB: I fear not; you must not risk so much, Master Edward. These Levelers spare nobody, and you had better let it be supposed that you are all burned in the house. If they think that, they will not come looking for you – or your sisters.

EDWARD: But my aunt knows the contrary, Jacob.

JACOB: Very true; I quite forgot that. *(Pausing)* Well, Master Edward, I will go to Lymington tomorrow and see the old lady; but you must remain here, and take charge of your sisters till I come back. Then we will consider what is to be done.

EDWARD: I understand. I will guard them with my life. Their safety is of the greatest importance.

JACOB: You will be safe here. This cottage is so well hidden. *(Gently)* The flames are not so bright as they were.

EDWARD: *(Stubbornly)* No. That must mean that there is little left to burn. It is my house that these Roundheads have burned down. *(Shaking his fists in the direction of the burning house)*

JACOB: It was your house, Master Edward, and it was your property, but how long it will be so remains to be seen. I fear that it will be forfeited. House or ruin – it will make no difference.

EDWARD: *(Angrily crying out)* Woe to the people who dare take possession of it! I shall be a man one of these days, if I survive this war. Then I will fight them. I will get back all my possessions. I will be a force to be reckoned with – and not just a worthless boy!

JACOB: Yes, Master Edward, and then you will reflect more than you do now, and not be rash. Let us go into the cottage, for it's no use remaining out in the cold; the frost is sharp tonight.

(JACOB goes into the cottage. EDWARD remains gazing at the distant, burning buildings)

EDWARD: *(To himself)* Reflect on my actions? Grow up and not be so rash? Oh Jacob, how little you really know me. I hate the Covenanters. They killed my father on the battlefield and now they have burned our property. One day I will take my revenge upon them. I do not yet know how, but my hand is ready to strike. I may still look like a boy but I have the heart and soul of a man. Tonight my dreams will be dreams of vengeance.

(He follows JACOB into the cottage)

by Frederick Marryatt, adapted by LAMDA

The Ride of Your Life

CHARLIE is a boy who owns a very unusual-looking dog, FITZ. Charlie is learning about Charles Darwin and evolution in school, but he struggles with his homework. One night, Fitz runs off to go on The Ride of Your Life, a fairground rollercoaster which goes back in time. Fitz manages to change his evolution so that he is much more handsome than before. Unfortunately, this change also alters Charlie's evolution, with disastrous results.

CHARLIE: FITZ! WHAT HAVE YOU DONE!

(Enter CHARLIE holding a duvet over his lower half)

FITZ: Hello master Charlie, the all-new Handsome Fitz at your service!

CHARLIE: Fitz. I can understand what you're saying. You can speak human!

FITZ: Isn't it wonderful master! Now we can be proper friends!

CHARLIE: And Fitz. You're so handsome.

FITZ: Who? *Moi?*

CHARLIE: Fitz.

FITZ: Yes master?

CHARLIE: *(Screams)* I'm going to kill you!

FITZ: But why master, I thought you'd be as happy as the happiest of happy things can be?

CHARLIE: Because of this!

(CHARLIE reveals his bottom half. He has turned into half boy, half fish)

FITZ: But master Charlie! You're half fish.

CHARLIE: I can see that you totally ugly and unnatural mutant who's suddenly become handsome.

FITZ: But I hate fish! Not as much as I hate worms but I hate them.

CHARLIE: How did this happen Fitz? What did you do? And why can you talk? And what are you wearing? I like the hat.

FITZ: Just a little trifle.

CHARLIE: Fitz! I'm half fish!

FITZ: Well look on the bright side master. I'm whole handsome with no more plum-pink bum that flashes like a Belisha beacon in the night. And the shock of the various transformations appears to have cured your flu!

CHARLIE: Ahhhhhhh-Choo!

FITZ: Well one out of two ain't bad.

CHARLIE: What did you do Fitz? Tell me the truth.

FITZ: Okay master. *(Fast)* I went to the park to The Ride of Your Life and it whooshed and it whirled and I went back in time and changed my evolution so I could be as handsome as me Mammy wanted me to be and now you've got a fishy tail and your mouth is doing strange fishy movements that are making me feel like I've done something really, really bad and that I'm going to be in deeply serious trouble.

CHARLIE: You changed evolution!

FITZ: Only a bit.

CHARLIE: You went back in time?

FITZ: Only a little.

CHARLIE: FITZ!

FITZ: Soz.

CHARLIE: Soz!

FITZ: Yes. Soz.

Continued ▸

CHARLIE: You've turned me into a fish Fitz and all you can say is "Soz"?!

FITZ: Half a fish.

CHARLIE: I'm going to kill you!

FITZ: But master how was I to know that by fiddling with my evolution I'd be fiddling in turn with yours? David Fattenborough said we were all one big family and I wanted to explain… Oh dear, all one big family. So if I changed my evolution then I changed…

CHARLIE: My evolution as well! Fitz. We have to change it back!

FITZ: But then I won't be the handsomest of all the handsome dogs. And I won't be able to speak human any more!

CHARLIE: I don't care Fitz!

FITZ: But it's what you wanted master, you said that sometimes you wished you could understand me so then we could be proper friends.

CHARLIE: I never said that.

FITZ: Yes you did!

CHARLIE: No I did not. Now, pick me up this instant and take me to The Ride of Your Life.

by Mick Gordon

Believe It Or Not

A is working in a bookshop when B comes in and asks for some rather mysterious advice.

A: Can I help you?

B: Yes. I'm looking for a book about ghosts.

A: We've got several titles to choose from. There's *The A to Z of Ghosts*, *The Supernatural World*, *Ghostfinder* and *Photographing Ghosts*.

B: I'll take them all.

A: Are you researching a book?

B: No. I think my house is haunted.

A: Really!

B: Yes, I've noticed some very strange things going on recently.

A: What sort of things?

B: Well, the other day I heard a strange noise coming from the loft. It was a sort of banging noise and then there's the lights.

A: What happens with the lights?

B: They flicker sometimes.

A: Oh! Have you been up to the loft to check?

B: Yes. I was terrified but I decided that I had to know what it was. I took a torch and went up there yesterday. What I saw made me decide to get some books on the subject.

A: What did you see?

B: It was a sort of glowing figure, leaning against the water tank.

Continued ▸

A: What sort of figure? A person?

B: Yes, I think so. It was looking straight at me. Just staring.

A: That must have been terrifying. Was it a man or a woman?

B: It's hard to say. It was dressed in rags, dirty rags.

A: What did you do?

B: I just froze. It was looking right at me. Then it pointed at the water tank. Then it spoke to me.

A: What did it say?

B: "Look in here." That's all it said.

A: Well, did you?

B: Would you?

A: I'm not sure. Not straight away. I'd have to think about it. What did you do?

B: I passed out.

A: What?

B: I fainted. I woke up about ten minutes later stretched out on my back in the loft. I was alone and very cold. It was very quiet.

A: What did you do next?

B: I got out of the loft quickly and made myself a cup of tea. I was very confused. I sat in the kitchen trying to gather my thoughts. Then about eleven at night I heard this tapping noise coming from the water pipes.

A: Couldn't that have been trapped air or something?

(Pause)

B: No, it was too regular. Like a rhythm. Three long taps followed by two short taps then two long taps. *(B demonstrates by tapping on the table)*

A: Morse code! That sounds like a Morse coded message.

B: I wrote it all down. *(Taking a piece of paper from his pocket and giving it to A)* I've written every long tap as a capital T and each short one as a small T.

A: Wait! I've got a book on Morse code somewhere. We can work out what it says. I won't be a moment.

(A exits. B looks to see that no one is watching then picks up the cash register and exits quickly. After a few seconds A returns reading aloud from a book)

A: I've worked out the code. It says 'Don't believe everything you hear'. *(Looks up and sees there is nobody there)* Where's he gone?

by Phil Jamieson

Level 2 Acting

Grade 4 Solo

Titles in Level 2 Acting: Grade 4 Solo

Son of Interflux

PHIL, Sam and Simon are best friends at an arts school in Long Island, New York. Simon's father is the senior vice-president of Interflux, a huge corporation whose expansion plans threaten the school's green space. Despite the family connection, Simon is leading the efforts to fight Interflux. On top of this, Phil's friends are now having girlfriend trouble, as Sam dates Barbara and Simon struggles with his feelings for Wendy. Phil is getting frustrated.

PHIL: *(Addressing Simon)* Sam? Oh, Sam's a boyfriend now. It happened this weekend, around the same time as Barbara became a girlfriend. That's the way it works. They come in pairs. Boyfriends never concern themselves with matters as trivial as fighting the corporation. All of their brain cells are taken up with thinking about the people they're boyfriends of. It's the same with girlfriends, only their brain cells are all taken up with making sure the boyfriends' brain cells are all taken up with the girlfriends.

No, I'm not jealous. This is not jealousy. It's aggravation. Get this. One date goes well, and Barbara, the timid little kid who can only worship from afar, gets cocky. You know what she did? She insulted the wreck! And what did Sam say? He said, "Yeah, I know. Phil and I have been thinking about getting a new one for a long time." Give me a break! This is *the wreck* we're talking about. The most beautiful, wonderful Volkswagen ever to rust, rattle and heave! He should have told her, "Listen, carrot-top, this is a great car. If you want to be driven around in a limo, well then *that's too bad*!" Let me tell you, this is a textbook case of boyfriend syndrome.

Continued ▸

Don't be surprised that Sam told Barbara that you like Wendy. It's just another symptom of boyfriend syndrome. And if I were you, I wouldn't say too much about this. You could be fighting off the effects of the same thing pretty soon, what with Wendy liking you and all. It's just bizarre enough for me to believe it. You and Wendy. Hmmm.

Sam has got it really bad. I've seen boyfriend syndrome before, but our man is really a victim. If you and Wendy get together, do me a favour and try to retain at least a little bit of the old Simon. This is a strange world. You think you know a guy, and zap! He turns into a boyfriend. Bing. The end.

by Gordon Korman, adapted by LAMDA

Ernie's Incredible Illucinations

ERNIE has been taken to see the doctor by his Mum and Dad because he has been having strange 'illucinations'. The doctor is seated at the side of the stage and produces a notebook. He is making notes on what follows.

ERNIE: *(To the doctor)* It started with these daydreams. You know, the sort everybody gets. Where you suddenly score a hat trick in the last five minutes of the Cup Final, or you bowl out the West Indies for ten runs – or saving your granny from a blazing helicopter, all that sort of rubbish. It was one wet Saturday afternoon and me and my mum and dad were all sitting about in the happy home having one of those exciting afternoon rave-ups we usually have in our house. *(He picks up a book and pretends to read)* It was all go. Mum thought Dad would be at the match. He didn't often miss a game but they were playing away. He told mum he was not going to Birmingham. Even for United.

Meanwhile – while this exciting discussion was in progress, I was reading this book about the French wartime resistance workers and the dangers they faced – often arrested in their homes. I started wondering what would happen if a squad of soldiers turned up at our front door, having been tipped off about the secret radio transmitter hidden in our cistern – when suddenly...

(He throws the book down, ceases talking directly to the doctor and becomes part of the scene he is describing. Looking around him) I can hear the tramp of feet. It's a squad of soldiers and they're marching up to our front door. They're banging on it now. I shouldn't go out there, Mum. I said don't go out there. It's not the milkman. It's a squad of enemy soldiers. They've come for me... The soldiers. They've found out about the radio transmitter. *(There is a loud crash)* Don't go out, Mum. Leave the television! Don't go! Mum...

Continued ▸

(Mum opens the door just as the two soldiers are charging. They shoot past her, straight into the hall, collide with ERNIE's Dad and land in a heap with him. Dad manages to hold the television above his head and save it from breaking. ERNIE crouches behind the table. To himself) They've surrounded the house. They want the television set. It's the neighbours' – not ours. They're forcing my Dad to go outside in the rain. They're threatening to shoot... *(Bursting out from behind the table)* Hold it! Drop those guns! *(As the officer raises his gun)* Da-da-da-da-da-da-da-da-da-da-da. *(The soldiers collapse and are strewn all over the hall. Mum screams. Then there is a silence)* Sorry, Mum. Yes, they are dead...

(ERNIE steps forward. As he speaks, and during the next section, Dad and Mum carry off the bodies)

Dad said it needed thinking about. It could have created a bit of gossip. And the carpet – it hadn't done that much good either. They didn't know what to do with the bodies. Well, Mum and Dad decided that the best thing to do was to pretend it hadn't happened. That was usually the way they coped with all emergencies...

by Alan Ayckbourn

In Control

LUCY is feeling dissatisfied with her boyfriend Gary, who never seems to stand up for himself. She thinks it may be time for her to break it off with Gary.

LUCY: This time I'm going to do it. Definitely. No weakness. Just finish it.

He comes in and I say: "Hello, Gary." Serious. Don't smile.

"You OK?" he'll ask.

"Yes, but I've something to say."

"Oh." And then he'll sit down, all attentive.

"Gary, it's over!" No no, too brutal. He'll just burst into tears.

"Gary, you know I like you, don't you, and you like me, and we like each other, both of us, together, the two of us, we've had some great times, smashing times, you and me, and…" Oh for goodness sake! He'll be asleep before I get to the good bit.

"Gary, I know we've been going out for three months, one week and two and a half days, but…" How did I know that? Can't say that, he'll think I'm still keen.

"Look, Gary – oh don't pull that little-boy-lost face. I'm trying to tell you something serious here. I don't want to … I know we… I don't…" Oh why is this so difficult? I don't want to hurt him. He's really nice but I don't feel anything for him. Why?

'Nice'. Yeah, 'nice'. That's the trouble. Too accommodating. Too soft. There's nothing exciting about him. Nothing challenging.

"For goodness sake, Gary, get some backbone. Stand up to me sometimes. Fight back."

Continued ▸

"But I don't want to fight you," he'll say. "I just want to make you happy."

"Then stop wimping round. I want a boyfriend, not a lap dog. Make some strong decisions, surprise me, make me respect you. Gary, don't just sit there, *do something*!"

(Her mobile rings)

Who's this? A text. 'Lucy, I'm bored with you. We're finished. Gary.' Bored? With *me*? I don't think so! Just wait till I see him. I'll give him a boring black eye with my boring handbag. *(Striding off)* This is what I call a relationship!

by Clifford Jury

Child of the Divide

BUTTAMEEZ and Pali are two boys caught up in the confusion following the partition of India and the creation of Pakistan. Buttameez is a Muslim and Pali is a Hindu by birth who has been brought up by a Muslim family in Pakistan. After several years, Pali's real father finds him again and wants to take him to India. Confused, Pali runs off to find his friend Buttameez – who lives in an old barn, as he does not have a home or family. In this scene, trying to give Pali advice, Buttameez tells him his own story.

BUTTAMEEZ: They'll be looking for you. They'll want to send you away. To your real family. At least you can get them back. You're lucky. This is my home. I sleep here. It can get very cold. Freezing in the winter. *(Shrugging his shoulders)* You can stay here if you want. I never told no one what happened to my family. Only the horses. The tonga-wallahs let me groom their horses for two annas. They give me food and let me stay here. I can speak to horses. You have to whisper to them and they answer you back. I trust them and they trust me. Can I trust you though? *(Hesitant as he tells his story)* All right then… First when the bullets started flying over our heads, it was pure fireworks… We'd play dodge-ball but it was like real bullets… People said the white goras had drawn a line on the map and now we had to go to a new country… Pakistan. I didn't wanna go, but there was no choice… Before we could leave, the mob came… I recognised our neighbour and Guddu's dad… Guddu was like my best friend, you know… We traded banter and swam in the river… My dad was brave… he could, like, actually mash someone if they even said something about his family… He just stood there… I saw them cut off his head and set fire to the house… I climbed to the roof and jumped into a pile of sugarcane chaff. They didn't see me… My legs. I didn't feel the pain. I just hid there, covered in

Continued ▸

sugarcane skins and licking them 'cos I was thirsty… and watched my family burn inside… They were screamin' and that… At night, I started walking straight… could hardly walk… kept asking people… "Where is Pakistan? Which way?" I crossed the border but I never saw no line. I'm no one's family. This old woman wanted me. She said her house was my house. I said I got no family, I don't need a house. And a schoolteacher said I could be his son but I didn't want to. I'm bad luck. Don't want to love anyone else. If you love people you lose them. *(Giving his quilt back to Pali)* Take it. I dried this for you.

by Sudha Bhuchar

Dogface

DOGFACE was attacked by a dog when she was seven, which causes the other children at school to provide her derogatory nickname – an identity she never fully escapes from. She alternates between describing the experience and reliving it.

DOGFACE: This is how it happens: One minute, you're just another awkward second-grader. And then your mom takes you and your brother to her friend's house, out in the country. You get out of the car, and there's a big yellow dog wagging his tail at you. And your mom and your brother go to ring the doorbell, and you get down on your knees in front of this friendly dog, and you're petting him… And then, suddenly, the dog snaps his jaws. And your life as you know it… ends.

The dog never barked, never growled. He followed after me, still friendly and playful. Blood pouring from the holes in my face… and he's looking at me, wagging his tail. My mother grabbed my jacket from the car, and told me to hold it tight against my face. I was crying. I was so panicked I felt like I was choking.

At the hospital, nurses were coming in, mopping up blood and asking questions and trying to establish how much of my face was still there, whether the nerve endings were alive. My face felt puffy and I was light-headed. The nurses were friendly, they wanted me to trust them. And I did. I believed them when they said that doctors would be able to fix me.

They lied. I was conscious the entire time. I was awake while they sewed my face back together. What I remember most is the bright light, and the strangely disembodied voices of my parents and the doctors, trying to keep the patient calm.

Continued ▸

When they finally let me see myself, when they gave me a mirror, I had prepared myself for a Halloween mask, for a horror movie, for a nightmare. But the blood had been cleaned away. It was just neat rows of stitches. I was actually relieved.

But then I went back to school. And then the real trauma began.

by Kellie Powell

Snow White and the Seven Dwarfs

The WICKED QUEEN is an intriguing character in the story of Snow White. She hates any opposition to her belief that she is the most beautiful woman in the world and will do anything, however cruel, to achieve this ambition. Her hatred of the lovely Snow White has become an obsession and she has unsuccessfully tried several ways to have her murdered. In this scene, the story has been placed in a contemporary context and the Wicked Queen has decided to enter a 'Miss World' beauty contest. She is speaking to the audience – but alternates between presenting her case as a contestant and reliving certain events in her life.

WICKED QUEEN: *(Entering with a dramatic flourish)* Well hello everybody, I'm here! I don't think you need to look any further for your Miss World. Why not save all the expense of a lavish show and just crown me now. Why am I so sure? Who are you, dear, and what do you know about beautiful women? Don't answer that, we haven't got time to waste. Well you see, I have a magic mirror, and it is able to see all the women in the world, and then report back to me who is the most beautiful. Every time I have asked it, well, apart from a little hiccup a while ago, every time it has told me that I am the most beautiful. What was the little hiccup? Oh some poor girl who was very lovely, but alas, *(she takes out her handkerchief)*, she had a most unfortunate accident. *(She pretends to weep)* I'm sorry, it does so upset me when I think of her. I have such a tender heart you see. I want peace and love for everyone all over the world. That is my sincere wish. What talents do I have? Well, I'm a very accomplished actress. Why, sometimes, to amuse my friends, I dress up as an old witch and they tell me I'm really convincing. *(She throws her scarf over her head and becomes the witch)* Have I got anything that you would like to buy, my dear? What about this pretty necklace? Yes, of course you can try it on. Because it's poisoned, you stupid little girl! *(Coming out of character)* Oh, sorry, I got a bit carried away there.

Continued ▸

Good though, aren't I? My figure is superb. My skin is as soft as satin and I never seem to age. I could go on being Miss World for years. And I have a very powerful effect on men. They do anything I say. See that one in the audience there, that handsome huntsman who is shaking in his boots. You would do anything I asked, wouldn't you? *Wouldn't you!* There, you see. Of course he does work for me, so he couldn't really disagree. So what are you waiting for? Do you want me as Miss World or not? I look wonderful in a swimsuit, I have enough money to pay off any of the other pathetic little candidates, and I could make life very difficult for all of you. What's that? My mirror! Who has brought that here? How dare you? It says what?! It's a fake! It's a fraud! *(She takes off her shoe and throws it at the mirror)* That's what I think of you, you stupid mirror. Now where's that huntsman gone? Come here. You've got some very serious questions to answer. Where are you?

by Eleanor McLeod

Beowulf

This is a story of a time long ago, of terrifying monsters and Beowulf, the hero, who kills them and brings to an end their reign of terror. In this scene, a runaway SLAVE comes across a group of Geats, members of Beowulf's own tribe, and tells them how, quite by chance, as he was running from his master, he discovered a sleeping dragon and hidden treasure.

SLAVE: I didn't mean to wake it. I was on the run. A slave, running from his master. I had no reason to run. My master's not a bad man. But it just got into me. Like a voice, nagging at me, day and night. Run, it said. Break loose. Be a free man. Those words, burning in me, like a fever. The only way to stop it was to run. So I ran, and I kept on running. I left behind the places where people lived, made for the wastes, where I wouldn't be found. Crags and boulders. Waves crashing over cliffs. And there, on the clifftop, a hill. Smooth and round. And a huge rock set in one side. There was a hole in the rock, just big enough to squeeze through. I crept inside, followed a low passageway sloping downwards. Then I saw a dim light ahead, glimmering in the dark. I went towards it, came to a stone doorway. The light came from beyond it, so I stepped through. And I was in a vast cavern and it was filled with gold.

It lay there before me. A huge creature, coiled beside the treasure. Its scales shone in the light of the gold. Or did the gold shine in the light of the scales? It didn't move. Its eyes were closed. It seemed to be sleeping. I crept closer. The heat that came off it! Like it was some kind of furnace. Water dripping from the roof rose up in clouds of steam. I reached my hand out towards it. I felt the power, the energy packed inside it. A little nearer and I could have touched it. My fingertips just that far off. I didn't touch it. I drew my hand back, crept out of the cavern, made my way back to the entrance.

Continued ▸

I was outside again, in sunlight and fresh air. I stood on the clifftop. I heard the sea below. And it was only then that I realised what I'd done. When I looked down I saw it. I swear I don't know how it got there. I don't remember taking it. But there it was, in my hand. A golden cup.

And the Dragon woke…

by David Calcutt

Under Hypnosis

BRENDA is a teenage girl whose mother has taken her to a hypnotist's show. In this scene, she becomes hypnotised and reveals more than she realises.

BRENDA: This is not where I want to be. Mum had a spare ticket to see this hypnotist and literally dragged me along with her. She loves his show on telly, she gets really excited about it. I'm not interested, I prefer *The X-Factor*, but when she said she'd buy me a new pair of boots, if I agreed to go with her, how could I refuse? So, here I am, ready to watch some idiots under hypnosis perform their monkey tricks.

If I snuggle down lower in my seat, no one is going to take any notice of me and I'll be able to doze off until it's all over. Now what's happening? *(Listens to a message over the loudspeaker)* Apparently a spotlight will fall on someone in the audience, who will then be the subject of tonight's show. Oh, please don't let that light fall on me. I promise I'll help more at home; I'll work harder in school – anything, only don't let… Too late. How embarrassing. Everyone in the world seems to be looking at me. *(She walks on to the stage and sits down)*

My name is Brenda and I live in Harlow. I'm here tonight with my Mum – under protest, I might add. I've never been hypnotised before and, to tell you the truth, I'm a bit nervous. Yes, I'm comfortable, thank you.

(She is immediately hypnotised and changes her manner and accent) Don't patronise me, I've told you countless times, I was nowhere near Tottenham on Saturday night. My boyfriend Sam asked me to go with him to the movies but I'd seen the film and wasn't keen to see it again, so we stayed at his place and watched a DVD. His parents were away for the weekend, so we had the place to ourselves. No, we didn't go to the High Street and we were not in

Continued ▸

the crowd that set fire to buildings and looted properties. What can I do to make you understand that we were at home during that time? CCTV? What do you mean? Well, it wasn't us. You have made a mistake. Teenagers all look the same. Besides you can't distinguish who's who when they're wearing hoodies. A picture? What picture? There must be a mistake. *(She looks at a picture)* That's not me – I don't even like those shoes. It isn't me. It isn't.

(Returning to her previous state) Have you started yet? You mean I've been hypnotised. Funny, I don't remember a thing. I hope it went well. I don't really believe in all this. It's just entertainment, isn't it?

by Jacqueline Stoker

Vanity Fair

It is the year 1815. BECKY Sharp and her richer, more ladylike friend, Amelia Sedley, are leaving Miss Pinkerton's Academy for young ladies in Chiswick. Amelia, loved and popular, will be sadly missed. Becky, a troublesome young woman, will not. She was taken on as an 'articled pupil' to speak French with the students and to receive her board and lodging. In this scene, the girls are on their way to Amelia's family where Becky has been invited to stay, before taking up a new post. They are in the carriage, having left Chiswick behind them.

BECKY: Thank God I'm out of Chiswick! Why, what's the matter, Amelia? Do you think Miss Pinkerton will come out and order me back to the black hole? I hate the whole house. I hope I may never set eyes on it again. I wish it were in the bottom of the Thames. O how I should like to see Miss Pinkerton floating in the water yonder, turban and all, with her train streaming after her, and her nose like the beak of a wherry… Hush, indeed, Amelia! Why, hush? Will the footman tell tales? He may go back and tell Miss Pinkerton that I hate her with all my soul, and I wish he would. For two years I have had only insults and outrage from her. I have been treated worse than any servant in the kitchen. I have never had a friend or a kind word, except from you. I have been made to tend to the little girls in the lower schoolroom and to talk French to the misses, until I got sick of my mother-tongue. But talking French to Miss Pinkerton was capital fun, wasn't it? She doesn't know a word of French, and was too proud to confess it! I believe it was that which made her part with me; and so thank heavens for French. *Vive la France! Vive l'Empereur! Vive Bonaparte!* It is no matter to me, Amelia, whether you should not have such wicked revengeful thoughts! Revenge may be wicked, but it's natural… and I'm no angel. I am most certainly not! Oh – there are too many deep carriage ruts on this road. I think the driver is going too fast! *(Pausing)* Are you looking forward to

Continued ▸

the future? You are very lucky Amelia. It must be delightful to have a family. Parents – kind, rich, affectionate parents who give you everything you ask for; and their love, which is more precious than all! My papa could give me nothing, and I had but two frocks in all the world! *(Smiling)* And then, to have a brother, a dear brother! Oh, how you must love him! Why, you are laughing! What! Don't you love him? You, who say you love everybody? I know you were only a little child when he went away. Isn't he very rich now? They say all Indian nabobs are enormously rich. And is your sister-in-law a nice, pretty woman? *(Pausing)* Not married? Not married! Ah, I had rather imagined that he would be. I mean, a man in his position would be expected to have a wife, wouldn't he?

(Aside) Maybe I can look forward to the future too! If Mr Joseph Sedley is rich and unmarried, why should I not marry him? I have only a fortnight, to be sure, but there is no harm in trying!

by William Makepeace Thackeray, adapted by LAMDA

Running

MARCUS is a teenage boy. He has been brought up by his father, who has been involved in a series of violent robberies. Marcus is unaware of his father's past criminal activities. One day, he returns home to find that his father and dog have been murdered. He tries to inform the police but disturbs the killers and has to run for his life. In this scene, Marcus is in hiding, trying to make sense of what is happening to him.

MARCUS: *(Runs in. Trying to catch his breath)* I think I've lost them for now. But they'll find me... they'll find me. I need to keep moving. *(Looking around)* I hope I'll be safe here for five minutes. I can't run any more for now.

(Covering his face) Now I know why my dad would never tell me what he did for work. Well, I guess I still don't know. And he can't tell me now.

(Looking around) What was that? They can't be here already... Surely not... *(Moves around the room, peers from behind the door)* No, nothing... I must have imagined it... But they'll be here soon. They're not going to stop now. *(Looking around)* What a weird place for me to end up. Something just told me to run here... My old school! This place has been abandoned for years, boarded up, but I figured I could just squeeze through one of those windows. So here I am. Hiding in Mrs Robertson's classroom... with a bunch of killers after me.

(Drawing in a shuddering breath) I was away over the weekend with friends. Camping. I was a bit mad at Dad though and didn't really want to see him when I got home. *(Covering his face again)* He'd been strange with me lately. Really, really strict. Always trying to tell me what to do – it was annoying. And as usual, he wouldn't tell me anything about what was going on in his life. We had a big fight about that and shouted at each other. I told him he should treat me like an adult, like an equal. He should be honest and let me into

Continued ▸

his world. And he said something… I'll never forget it now. He said "You don't want to be part of my world." He looked really sad when he said that. *(Almost crying)* And then I went away for the weekend. I can't believe that the last time I saw him, I was mad at him. I'll never be able to fix that now.

I came home. I walked from Andy's house because it's just around the corner. Our house was all dark and then… I saw the dog. Dead, on the front steps. And then I saw that the front door was open… I rushed inside… and Dad… *(Choking)* It was pretty obvious that he was gone… I called the police and told them what happened. And a second after I got off the phone with the police… I heard the first gunshot. Right there in the kitchen. The bullet broke the window and went past my head. I ran out the back door and started climbing the fence. When I looked back, there were at least three of them… dressed in black and with the biggest guns I've ever seen in my life, even in the movies. I was in shock but I jumped over the fence and just ran… What am I going to do? Dad, I wish you were here!

(Raises head quickly as though he hears a door slam) They're here.

by Clarissa Aykroyd

Grade 4 Duologue

Titles in Level 2 Acting: Grade 4 Duologue

Ruckus in the Garden

The students of two schools, the rough-and-tumble Riverdale Comprehensive School and the upper-class St Nectan's Grant-Maintained Secondary School, encounter each other on school trips to visit a historic garden. Conflicts and romance quickly arise. In this scene, MAISY from St Nectan's and ROCK from Riverdale meet each other for the first time.

(MAISY is crawling through the undergrowth)

MAISY: I got away. Dived through a camellia and crawled round the Temple of Flora. Two Riverdale boys were pinning a St Nectan's ninth-year up against a statue of Vulcan. It was horrible. I just want to find somewhere quiet to finish *Middlemarch*.

(She almost literally bumps into ROCK, who is crawling in terror in the other direction. Both scream and recoil)

Aaaah!

ROCK: Don't kill me! Please don't kill me!

(Beat. They look at each other)

MAISY: Are you from Riverdale?

ROCK: Are you from St Nectan's?

MAISY: Are you alone?

(ROCK nods)

ROCK: You?

MAISY: *(Nods)* Are you going to shout for help?

ROCK: Are you?

(Beat)

MAISY: What's your name?

Continued ▸

ROCK: My name is Tim but everyone calls me Rock.

MAISY: Why do they call you Rock?

ROCK: Because I'm the puniest boy in Riverdale. It's kind of a joke.

MAISY: You shouldn't have told me that. I'm going to beat you up now.

(Beat. ROCK gets scared)

That was a joke too.

ROCK: Oh, right.

MAISY: Nice to meet you, Rock. I'm Maisy.

ROCK: What are you doing in the camellias?

MAISY: I was trying to find somewhere to read.

ROCK: Read what?

MAISY: *Middlemarch*. It's a novel by George Eliot.

ROCK: Never heard of him.

MAISY: It's a woman, silly. She writes about a nineteenth-century woman who is trapped by her society into marrying for respectability rather than for love. George Eliot is my second favourite author.

(Beat)

Aren't you going to ask who my favourite author is?

ROCK: Go on then.

MAISY: It's Jane Austen. My favourite book is *Emma*. And my favourite character is Mr Knightley.

ROCK: What's he like, then.

MAISY: He's quiet, unassuming and in some ways shy, but with an inner moral integrity that Emma finally finds irresistible.

ROCK: I don't read books much.

MAISY: I blame the decline of the lending library.

ROCK: Just never really got into it.

MAISY: I could read to you.

ROCK: What, now?

MAISY: Neither of us want to fight. We could just stay here until it's time to go back to the coaches and I could read to you from *Middlemarch*.

ROCK: Suppose.

MAISY: Well, I won't bother if you're not interested. You try to bring a bit of literature into their lives…

ROCK: No. I want to. It's just… if they see us…

MAISY: I'll say you were holding me hostage. You caught me and dragged me in here and roughed me up something dreadful.

ROCK: Really?

(MAISY deliberately roughs up her uniform so it looks like she's been pushed around)

MAISY: How's that? Vulnerable enough?

ROCK: It's great.

MAISY: You did that. You heathen. *(Suddenly prosaic)* Come over here then. I won't bite.

(He approaches her cautiously)

We're nearly the same height.

ROCK: I hate being little.

MAISY: It's good for hiding under camellias. Now I'm already on chapter twenty-seven, so I need to start by giving you a summary of the story so far… Dorothea, a passionate young woman in search of a belief system to match the agitation of her mind, marries the dark and skeletal figure of Mr Casaubon…

by David Farr

Ostrich Boys

KENNY, BLAKE and Sim have stolen the ashes of their recently deceased friend Ross, intending to take them to the village of Ross in Scotland. Along the way they are pursued by the police and other adults, manage to lose bags and tickets, and meet three girls, Kat, Hayley and Kayleigh. All the while, they are trying to face up to the reasons for Ross's death. As they get close to their final destination, Kenny and Sim have dropped out and Blake has gone on alone.

KENNY: Blake!... Blake!

(BLAKE waves to him, beckoning him over)

BLAKE: You seem to be making a habit of reappearing. How'd you get here?

KENNY: Kat's stepdad.

BLAKE: I don't understand.

KENNY: *(Shows BLAKE the back of his hand, where a phone number is written)* I was looking for a bus stop. *(Shrugs)* Then I saw this phone box, and, you know... But I've had to tell her the truth. She knew most of it anyway – because of the telly?

BLAKE: Where is she now?

KENNY: They're waiting in their car by the road.

BLAKE: What made you change your mind? Why'd you come? *(Pause)* I'm really glad you're here. Genuinely. I just wondered why. Because you could have called your mum.

KENNY: I knew you'd come. I hoped Sim would too. Is he...?

(BLAKE shakes his head)

KENNY: So what do we do now?

BLAKE: Honestly? I haven't got a clue.

KENNY: I think what you say is true. I think Ross did, you know, do it on purpose. But then, I also can't believe he really would do it either. I knew him the longest – I knew him for ever – and it's just not like the Ross I knew would ever do that. Do you think it's our fault he did?

BLAKE: Some of it. But I don't think we'd have been able to stop him either.

KENNY: Maybe if he'd told us how he felt.

BLAKE: Maybe. But he never would have, would he? He was one of those people who are good at hiding everything inside – everything that really mattered to him anyway.

KENNY: But why did he do it by getting run over?

BLAKE: Because he didn't want anybody to know. I reckon that's why he tried to cover up that he'd been to those Internet chatrooms. He was still trying to hide everything inside right up until the end.

KENNY: Yeah, but doing that meant we couldn't help him.

BLAKE: He didn't think he wanted help. He just thought he wanted to die.

KENNY: I don't want him gone. He was my best friend. I want him here. He should *still* be here. You know, yesterday and today have been amazing. All the stuff we've been through. And it's all been because of him. I'm telling you, we've got the best story ever. But he missed out. He's never going to be able to tell it. *(Pause)* Do you think Sim's going to come?

BLAKE: No. Not now.

KENNY: Why not?

BLAKE: Don't take this the wrong way, but I think Ross broke his heart. I think Sim looked up to Ross more than any of us. And I bet if Sim could have swapped lives with someone, he would have jumped at the chance of being Ross for a while. He can't understand why Ross would want to throw everything away.

Continued ▸

KENNY: Nor me.

BLAKE: I reckon it's probably me and you from here on in. I hate to say it, but don't be surprised if we don't see much of Sim any more. I hope I'm wrong, but…

KENNY: But you're probably not. *(Taking the urn)* So what do we do with him?

BLAKE: I don't know. I've been thinking it wouldn't be fair to his mum or dad if we left him here, would it? We've been blaming them all along, but… but I can't think of *anybody* who is blameless any more.

KENNY: Maybe we should just leave a little bit here, but take the rest back. We can't come all this way and then not do something.

(KENNY unscrews the lid and throws a small scoop of ash toward the lighthouse. BLAKE repeats the action. The boys stand in silence)

BLAKE: *(Suddenly breaking the silence)* Listen! Can you hear anything? It's a car!

KENNY: Someone's grassed us up. Do you reckon it was Sim?

BLAKE: I don't know. I doubt it. Maybe they just figured it out because someone local spotted us. We've left a pretty obvious trail all the way from Cleethorpes … Here we go. Brace yourself.

KENNY: There is something I will tell you. I'm not glad Ross is dead, okay? You know that, don't you? But I can't help being glad we came here. I wouldn't have met Kat if we hadn't.

BLAKE: I suppose when you think about it, that's kind of the whole point, isn't it?

KENNY: How do you mean?

BLAKE: Well, you never really know what's going to happen, do you? At least, not until it actually does.

by Keith Gray, adapted by LAMDA

The Mirror

LINDA and JOYCE are two girls who have never met before. They are alone in their respective bedrooms, feeling gloomy about how uneventful their lives are. Suddenly, they find themselves talking to each other in a very unexpected way.

LINDA AND JOYCE: Nothing exciting ever happens to me.

(Both go to mirror to contemplate image)

LINDA: *(Surprised)* I look terrible.

JOYCE: You're telling me.

LINDA: Hey!

JOYCE: Hey!

(Each puts a hand to the mirror. They rotate their hands, one against the other, synchronized, as though touching the mirror)

LINDA: You're not me.

JOYCE: Thank goodness for that.

LINDA: Well, get out of my mirror!

JOYCE: I'm not in anything, except my bedroom. You're the one who's stuck in the mirror. *(Pause)* Isn't it cramped?

LINDA: Very funny. Listen. I've got a date tonight, and even though it's with boring old Arnold I want to look good. So get lost and send me, or whoever it is that's supposed to be in there, back.

JOYCE: This is out of my hands. Honest. It's never happened before. Are you sure you're not a piece of glass?

LINDA: Don't get insulting. *(Pause)* Hmmm. This is kind of interesting you know?

JOYCE: *(Aside)* Not from my perspective.

Continued ▸

LINDA: I bet I know what's going on. You're my alter ego, sent here to help me learn about myself. That's it. Turn around.

JOYCE: What?

LINDA: Turn around. I want to see what my other side looks like.

(JOYCE shrugs and turns around slowly)

LINDA: Boy, am I in bad shape.

JOYCE: *(Indignant)* Hey!

LINDA: No offense. But I...you, could lose a few pounds.

JOYCE: How would you like to lose a few teeth?

LINDA: Try it. How can you reach me?

JOYCE: *(Puts both hands against the mirror but can't push through)* You're right. So, what are we going to do? Just stand here and criticize each other?

LINDA: No, that would be a waste of a valuable opportunity. This thing... whatever it is that's going on, might not last very long. We should make good use of the time.

JOYCE: *(To herself)* Maybe if I went back to bed and got up tomorrow.

LINDA: Are you listening to me?

JOYCE: Yes, yes. But I don't see much good coming of this.

LINDA: Don't you? By exploring our opposites we can get to know ourselves better.

JOYCE: Who cares?

LINDA: Well. I'm already learning something.

JOYCE: *(Suspiciously)* Like what?

LINDA: Like, I'm inquisitive and you're not. Say, are you going on a date tonight, too?

JOYCE: Forget it. I'd rather go horseback riding.

LINDA: You're kidding.

JOYCE: No. A Horse doesn't talk back.

LINDA: *(Considers this)* That's true. *(Pause)* But then again, I don't have to worry about Arnold kicking me in the head. And I don't have to feed him every day.

JOYCE: *(Brusquely)* Okay. Okay. We both have reasons for keeping the company we do. So what?

LINDA: *(Shrugs, a little hurt. Tentatively)* Do you like to go dancing?

JOYCE: No. Bowling.

LINDA: Do you like long dresses?

JOYCE: Jeans.

LINDA: Chopin?

JOYCE: The Plastic Slugs.

LINDA: *(Sighs)* Favorite color?

JOYCE: *(Bored)* Blue.

LINDA: What? Blue? But that's mine, too. Hunh. So that means that even though we're different, we're not exact opposites. Let's try to keep going. Please?

JOYCE: *(Pause. Grudgingly)* Okay.

LINDA: Terrific! Favorite season?

JOYCE: Spring.

LINDA: Mine, too! Favorite flower?

JOYCE: Tulip.

LINDA: Yes! Favorite time of day?

JOYCE: *(Getting interested)* Morning.

Continued ▸

LINDA: Favorite smell?

JOYCE: *(Excited)* Bread baking.

LINDA: This is wonderful! Favorite sound?

JOYCE: Birds singing.

LINDA: *(Closes her eyes and spreads out her arms, caught up in the moment)* Favorite food?

JOYCE: *(Hugging herself)* Stewed tomatoes!

(LINDA gasps. Holds stomach. Makes gagging sounds)

(Archly.) You have a problem with stewed tomatoes?

LINDA: I'm sorry. I was just expecting something more along the lines of ice cream… cake… You know, we're actually getting along better than I thought we would.

JOYCE: Um, I'm sorry if I snapped at you earlier. This has been kind of fun.

LINDA: Oh, that's okay. I think this whole mirror deal sort of threw us.

JOYCE: Yeah. The mirror. I forgot you're not really here, over here with me. *(Shrugs. Grudgingly)* I almost wish you could be. Over here, that is.

LINDA: *(Laughs lightly)* No. No, it would never work out.

JOYCE: *(Turns away)* I'm going now.

LINDA: What do you mean? Going where?

JOYCE: Out of my room so I won't have to look at me… you… the mirror!

LINDA: Wait! Wait! Don't go.

JOYCE: *(Considers)* Well, okay. *(Impulsively)* Shake.

(They try to shake hands but the mirror prevents them)

LINDA: Um… let's just wave at each other.

(They wave)

JOYCE: I wonder when we'll get our mirrors back.

LINDA: I don't know. You know, this could be permanent.

JOYCE: Permanent? Now wait a minute. I like a little privacy in my bedroom. Not that I have weird habits, you understand. Hey, you're getting fuzzy.

LINDA: We could see how we grow up and change.

JOYCE: Listen! Listen to me! You're fading away. And I can hardly hear you.

LINDA: Me, as a successful scientist. You, as a famous showjumper.

JOYCE: Hello?! Hello?! She's gone.

LINDA: *(Turns to mirror. Face falls)* She's gone.

(LINDA and JOYCE approach the mirror. Slowly they raise their right hands. Wave)

LINDA AND JOYCE: Bye.

by Joseph McNair Stover

The Haunting of Ebenezer Scrooge

On Christmas Eve the miserly old SCROOGE locks up his counting house and retires to his room, where he locks himself in. He sits over a low fire, taking his gruel before going to bed and complaining to himself about the wasteful, unnecessary frivolities of Christmastime. He does not know that he is about to have a frightening encounter with the GHOST of his former business partner, Jacob Marley.

SCROOGE: Merry Christmas! Happy New Year! Humbug! The world's mad. *(He starts)* What's that? Imagination, indigestion! Now *I'm* mad. More humbug! *(Listens)* Eh? *(Goes to the door and listens with his ear against the panel)* Nothing! *(Starts to walk back to his chair but freezes halfway there. Listens again, and slowly turns in terror to the door as he hears something. Moves back from the door as his face and gestures reveal that what he has heard is getting louder, coming closer. He cowers down to the floor. Suddenly)* Marley's ghost! *(Screams)*

(As SCROOGE screams the ghost of Jacob Marley enters)

How now! What do you want with me?

GHOST: Much!

SCROOGE: Marley's voice! Who are you?

GHOST: Ask me who I *was*.

SCROOGE: Who *were* you, then? *(Getting some of his old cantankerous spirit back)* You're very particular, for a shade.

GHOST: In life I was your partner, Jacob Marley.

SCROOGE: Can you – can you sit down?

GHOST: I can.

SCROOGE: Do it then.

GHOST: You don't believe in me?

SCROOGE: I don't.

GHOST: Why do you doubt your senses?

SCROOGE: Because the smallest thing affects them. A slight disorder of the stomach makes them cheats. You may be an undigested bit of beef, a blot of mustard or a crumb of cheese. *(Cackles)* There's more of gravy than of a grave about you, whatever you are! You're humbug, I tell you. Humbug!

(The GHOST rises and spreads its arms, wailing, then slowly subsides)

Mercy! Mercy! Dreadful apparition, why do you trouble me?

GHOST: Man of worldly mind, do you believe in me or not?

SCROOGE: I do. I must. But why do spirits walk the earth, and why do they come to me?

GHOST: It is required of every man that his spirit should walk abroad among his fellows. If that spirit goes not forth in life, it is condemned to do so after death – to witness what it cannot share, but might have shared on earth. *(Another terrible cry)*

SCROOGE: *(Trembling)* You are fettered! Tell me why?

GHOST: I wear the chain I forged in life, link by link and yard by yard. Would you know the weight and length of the strong chain you bear yourself? Yours is a ponderous chain, Ebenezer Scrooge!

SCROOGE: Jacob! Old Jacob Marley, tell me more! Speak comfort to me, Jacob!

GHOST: I have none to give. It comes from other regions, and is conveyed by other ministers to other kinds of men. I cannot rest, I cannot stay. In life my spirit never moved beyond our counting house, and weary journeys now lie before me.

SCROOGE: You must have been very slow about them, Jacob.

GHOST: Slow!

Continued ▸

SCROOGE: Seven years dead, and travelling all the time?

GHOST: The whole time! On the wings of the wind. No rest, no peace. Incessant torture of remorse! Oh, captive, bound and double-ironed – not to know that no space of regret can make amends for a life of opportunities misused! Yet such was I! Oh, such was I!

SCROOGE: But you were always a good man of business, Jacob.

GHOST: Business! Mankind should have been my business. Charity, mercy, forbearance and benevolence were my proper business. The dealings of my trade were but a drop of water in the comprehensive ocean of my business! At this time of the rolling year I suffer most. Why did I walk with my eyes turned down and never raise them to that blessed star which led the Wise Men to a poor abode?

SCROOGE: Don't be hard on me! Don't be flowery, Jacob, pray!

GHOST: Hear me! I have sat invisible beside you, many and many a day. *(SCROOGE shivers)* That was no light part of my penance. I am here tonight to warn you that you have yet a chance and hope of escaping my fate. A chance and hope of *my* procuring, Ebenezer.

SCROOGE: You were always a good friend to me. Thankee, Jacob.

GHOST: You will be haunted by Three Spirits.

SCROOGE: Is that the chance and hope you mentioned, Jacob?

GHOST: It is.

SCROOGE: I – I think I'd rather not.

GHOST: Without their visits you cannot hope to shun the path I tread. Expect the first spirit tomorrow when the bell tolls one.

SCROOGE: Couldn't I take 'em all at once, and have it over, Jacob?

GHOST: You must take them as *you* made them, Ebenezer, for the first spirit is the Ghost of Christmas Past – *your* past!

SCROOGE: And then, Jacob, what then?

GHOST: Expect the second on the next night at the same hour. The Ghost of Christmas Present – *your* present!

SCROOGE: And after that phantom – what is the third?

GHOST: The third comes upon the next night, when the last stroke of twelve has ceased to vibrate. The Ghost of Christmas Yet To Come! He is your hope, Ebenezer. Mark him well! Look to see me no more. And look that, for your own sake, you remember what has passed between us! Learn, learn! Learn from the shades of Christmas Past and Christmas Present how you must live for a Christmas Yet To Come!

(The GHOST rises, wraps its mantle about its head and starts to back away. SCROOGE sits forward on his chair, watching. The GHOST beckons him. SCROOGE approaches to within two paces, when the GHOST holds up his hands, warning him to come no nearer. SCROOGE covers his eyes and bows his head.

The GHOST exits.

SCROOGE drops his hands and darts looks around him. Then he moves quickly to the door, tries it to make sure it is still locked, goes centre and pauses and listens. He returns to his chair and sinks into it. Then he jerks upright)

SCROOGE: Humbu…! *(He looks fearfully round and sinks back into his chair)*

by Charles Dickens,
adapted by Maureen Blythe from A Christmas Carol

The Maze

CHRIS and JO are on a school visit to Headstone Manor. They have been given half an hour free time to explore by themselves before meeting up with the other members of their class at a designated rendezvous. They have been told that they can go anywhere as long as they are not late back… and as long as they don't go anywhere near the maze.

(CHRIS and JO enter, looking at a map and a brochure of the Manor and its gardens)

CHRIS: *(Looking around)* Here we are! Tall hedges and a narrow entrance. We've found it. This must be the maze!

JO: We really shouldn't go in. Mr Patel said we could go anywhere *but* the maze. We've found it now – let's go back to the gift shop.

CHRIS: *(Going over to the entrance and reading)* It says here that 'the maze was designed in 1705 by George London and Henry Wise, who created the maze at Hampton Court Palace for William III.' It goes on to say that Sir Horatio Headstone commissioned 'a similar Puzzle maze for Headstone Manor.' That's really interesting.

JO: What's a Puzzle maze?

CHRIS: That's simple. *(Continues reading)* 'A Puzzle maze has more than one path.'

JO: Mmm. More than one way to get lost, you mean.

CHRIS: Oh, come on!

JO: Perhaps we should go back. We haven't got time to explore. We were told *not* to come here…

CHRIS: Since when has that stopped you doing anything! We *won't* have time if you stand here arguing.

JO: Well… it's dark in there… and people get lost… and… you could be stuck in there for days and no one would find you… and it's supposed to be haunted… and…

CHRIS: *(Dragging JO by the arm)* Come on! No more excuses. Let's go! Anyway, I'll go on my own if you won't come too. It can't be that difficult. *(Walks off into the maze)*

JO: Chris! Wait! Wait for me! Don't go without me…

(JO follows in the direction in which CHRIS has run. They follow a pattern of imaginary hedges, placed around the acting area)

CHRIS: *(Turning around)* I *knew* you'd want to come! Now, stay right behind me. We don't want to get separated.

JO: This is a dead end. We've got to choose left or right. How do we know which path?

CHRIS: We don't… but that's the fun of it… and this *is* fun, you know. Much better than ordinary lessons.

JO: It's a kind of history lesson though – especially in the house. Wish *I* had a four poster bed!

CHRIS: Let's concentrate. *(Getting a coin out)* 'Heads' we go left – 'tails' we go right. *(Flips the coin)*

JO: *(Picking it up)* Tails!

CHRIS: 'Right' it is… Follow me!

(CHRIS takes a right turn and again follows an imaginary line of hedges. JO follows. From time to time they try to peer over the hedge, but they are just not tall enough to see anything)

JO: *(Jumping up to try and look over the hedge)* I can't see where we are or where we are going.

CHRIS: It's such a thick hedge.

JO: I give up. I'm going back.

Continued ▸

CHRIS: Please yourself – but you won't find the way out.

JO: Oh yes I will! I've left a trail.

CHRIS: *(Turning around)* A trail? What do you mean?

JO: Just what I said – I've left a trail of sweets. I've been dropping them along the path. I didn't tell you because I thought you'd laugh at me.

CHRIS: *(Laughing)* I've never heard anything so stupid. A trail... yes, but sweets! They'll be so small, you'll never find them.

JO: *(Flouncing away)* I will! Just you wait and see. I'll be eating an ice-cream back at the shop while you are still wandering around in here.

(Both move away from each other, following the imaginary lines of the maze. JO is concentrating on looking for the sweet trail and CHRIS is trying to follow a path which may lead to the centre of the maze)

CHRIS: It can't be far now! Only another corner and... *(Moves around a hedge to find nothing but a dead end)* Oh no! The path finishes here. It's another dead end. I must have taken a wrong turn.

JO: *(Scrabbling on the ground)* I can't find any of them! Chris was right, like always. It *was* a silly idea. I was sure this was the way we came in.

(Both continue to follow the imaginary lines of the maze, but, of course, cannot see each other and are getting worried and concerned about their lack of progress)

CHRIS: I wish Jo hadn't gone back.

JO: I wish Chris was here. It's getting darker now. I hate these tall hedges. We've been so long, somebody must have missed us by now. *(Calling out)* Chris! Chris can you hear me?

CHRIS: *(Trying to peer over the top of a hedge)* Jo? Is that you?

JO: *(Trying to work out the direction of the sound)* Chris! Chris!

CHRIS: I can hear you Jo.

JO: Are you in the middle yet?

CHRIS: No! I seem to be going round in circles.

JO: My sweet trail didn't work either.

CHRIS: *(Speaking louder)* What did you say?

JO: *(Speaking louder)* My sweet trail didn't work.

CHRIS: Let's try and find each other.

JO: How can we do that?

CHRIS: Make noises... and we follow the sounds.

JO: What a brilliant idea.

CHRIS: You first.

JO: I could try phoning your mobile?

CHRIS: You could... but the battery's flat!

JO: *(Loudly)* Hallooooooo... Hallooooooo... Hallooooooo!

CHRIS: *(In an undertone)* I think it's coming from that direction. *(Moves a few paces to the left and round the other side of a hedge)*

JO: *(Even louder)* Halloooo... Halloooo... Hallooooo! *(In an undertone)* I'm not going to just stand here and make stupid noises. The calls seemed to come from over there. No... wait... was it over there *(Pointing in another direction)* ... or even there?

CHRIS: *(Calling out)* Come on. I can't hear you, Jo!

JO: *(Louder still)* Halloooo... Hallooooo... Hallooooo!

CHRIS: *(Listening carefully)* Got it!

JO: *(Listening carefully)* This way!

(Both make a final move through the maze and find themselves facing each other, back at the entrance... where they started)

Continued ▸

CHRIS: *(Speaking together)* Jo!

JO: *(Speaking together)* Chris!

(They hug each other)

JO: I'm so glad to see you.

CHRIS: We shouldn't have separated. *(Looking around them)* And guess what?

JO: We're back where we started!

CHRIS: Oh Jo… Look… over there… coming towards us!

JO: It's Mr Patel and there's someone with him.

CHRIS: Miss Maloney.

JO: The Headmistress!

CHRIS: I think we're in trouble.

JO: We are rather late.

CHRIS: They must have missed us!

CHRIS AND JO: *(Together)* Hello Miss… Hello Sir!

by Jacqueline Emery

All Stops Out

Teenage students in Australia are facing up to the pressures of the HSC exam, which will help to determine whether they graduate from high school. In this scene, LINDA and JENNY, who are in a detention centre for young offenders, are arguing over whether it is a waste of time to try to further their education. Linda is doing her best to bully Jenny into submission.

LINDA: How come you disappeared?

JENNY: Felt tired.

LINDA: The game was getting really interesting.

JENNY: Wanted to lie down.

LINDA: Don't you like pool?

JENNY: Yes. It's a good game.

LINDA: So why didn't you stay and watch? You aren't going to learn sitting in here all the time.

JENNY: I felt homesick.

LINDA: You didn't watch the game Tuesday either. You tired then?

JENNY: I wanted to write a letter.

LINDA: To your beloved?

JENNY: Mum and Dad.

LINDA: But you shouldn't just walk out in the middle of a game like that.

JENNY: Sorry.

LINDA: This place is full of very suspicious people, you know. They might start to worry. They might get a bit edgy.

Continued ▸

JENNY: I'll make sure it doesn't –

LINDA: Might think you're doing something secret, that you don't want anyone else to know about.

JENNY: Like what?

LINDA: Like reading that book you've stuffed under the mattress. Give it to me.

JENNY: I just picked it up when I came back to lie down.

LINDA: Give it to me.

JENNY: It doesn't really interest me. You're right about everything being stuffed. I mean what's the point of studying and stuff like that? I mean there isn't any is there.

LINDA: Didn't I tell you I didn't want to see this stuff in here ever again.

JENNY: Yes.

LINDA: So what's it doing here?

JENNY: I was reading it.

LINDA: Were you?

JENNY: The social worker's arranging for me to sit the exam. I thought I may as well do it.

LINDA: I don't think that's really such a good idea. I think The Saint is just sticking her nose in where it's not really wanted. Don't you reckon?

JENNY: Yeah.

LINDA: So maybe you should tell her you're not really all that interested in doing this HSC. She'll understand. Social workers are very understanding people, when are you seeing her again?

JENNY: She's coming in at the end of the week.

LINDA: You can tell her then. Can't you?

JENNY: Yes.

LINDA: Good. Got that cleared up really well, didn't we. We can go back to the game now. And we can drop this useless book off at the incinerator on the way there.

JENNY: What are you afraid of?

LINDA: Who's afraid?

JENNY: Are you afraid of books? The very first time you saw this textbook you went a bit pale. Do they frighten you?

LINDA: No.

JENNY: Why won't you let me study?

LINDA: I don't want you wasting your time.

JENNY: That's not a reason. You are afraid.

LINDA: I'm not.

JENNY: You're afraid I might end up a bit intelligent.

LINDA: Bull.

JENNY: Here. Look inside the book. Is that what makes you so upset? A few diagrams? Bit of writing?

LINDA: I'm going to the rec. room.

JENNY: You're afraid. That's why you're trying to stand over me. I bet everyone who comes near you has to stay the way they are or else you get frightened. You're terrified I won't end up like you.

LINDA: You already have. You're in here.

JENNY: But I'll get out again.

LINDA: Yeah, and you'll end up straight back in again, everyone does. Once you walk through the door of a place like this you can bet you'll never leave.

JENNY: I will.

LINDA: Forget it.

Continued ▸

JENNY: I'll try.

LINDA: What for?

JENNY: Because.

LINDA: Moron.

JENNY: I'm not a moron. And I'm not going to try and become one, like you. This stuff is interesting. I can't stop myself from being interested. So I'm going to read it. Right? Even if it gets me nowhere, I'm going to read it. Right? *(Silence)* Right?

LINDA: Do what you like.

JENNY: I will.

LINDA: Good.

JENNY: So leave me alone. I'm going to study.

LINDA: Great.

JENNY: Now.

LINDA: Good on you.

by Michael Gow

Acting Class

CRYSTAL is taking acting classes. Her TEACHER is faced with the considerable challenge of keeping Crystal focused, and helping her to find inspiration.

TEACHER: Now then Crystal, you say you've done this piece before, so let's have a big, big performance shall we, sweetheart? Lots of life, lots of energy – fill the room with your glorious voice. That's it darling, stand tall and proud, and…

CRYSTAL: *(Very mechanically)* O – for – a – fuse – of – wire – that – would – send – the – highest – heaven – of – intention. I'm going to a party tonight.

TEACHER: Are you, darling? That's lovely. Now then. The words are so nearly, nearly there. *Muse of fire*. Can you remember what a muse is?

CRYSTAL: Is it a camel?

TEACHER: Nnnooo. Not really. It's inspiration isn't it? Something that fills us with imagination. And *invention* darling, which is…?

CRYSTAL: Is that a camel?

TEACHER: No, not a – where are you getting all this camel stuff from?

CRYSTAL: We've been doing transport through the ages.

TEACHER: Oh.

CRYSTAL: Did you know a camel can fly twice round the earth without eating?

TEACHER: A camel? Are you sure?

CRYSTAL: Miss Taylor said.

Continued ▸

TEACHER: Well, just check that before you commit pen to paper. Now then. We've got the right words, let's *perform* them. Imagine you have a great big audience eager to hear you explode into life. And…

CRYSTAL: O – for – a – fuse –

TEACHER: Muse.

CRYSTAL: muse – of – fire – that – can –

TEACHER: Would.

CRYSTAL: would – attend –

TEACHER: Ascend.

CRYSTAL: ascend – the – biggest –

TEACHER: Brightest.

CRYSTAL: brightest – heaven – of – injection –

TEACHER: Vention.

CRYSTAL: invention.

TEACHER: Well… that was our one step back, wasn't it? Now let's have two great big steps forward.

CRYSTAL: My mum's a teacher.

TEACHER: Is she?

CRYSTAL: Only she teaches at night. Sometimes *all* night.

TEACHER: I see. What does daddy do?

CRYSTAL: He's in prison.

TEACHER: Oh, right.

CRYSTAL: I'm going to Kirsty's party tonight.

TEACHER: That will be lovely. Is she your best friend?

CRYSTAL: O – for – a – muse – of – fire – that – would – ascend – the – brightest – heaven – of – invention.

TEACHER: That's wonderful darling. Word perfect. Good girl. So now you *know* the words, we need to *sing* them out.

CRYSTAL: O – for – a –

TEACHER: Sing them sweetheart: O for a –

CRYSTAL: O – for – a – muse –

TEACHER: Muse of invention –

CRYSTAL: That – would – ascend –

TEACHER: Ascend!

CRYSTAL: Ascend.

TEACHER: *Ascend* darling, like the lark, rise up, up to the sky, *ascend*!

CRYSTAL: Ascend – the – brightest – heaven –

TEACHER: Heaven of invention!

CRYSTAL: Of – invention.

TEACHER: Crystal, petal, whose idea was it to do this piece?

CRYSTAL: My old teacher.

TEACHER: And what happened to –

CRYSTAL: He wasn't a real teacher.

TEACHER: Oh.

CRYSTAL: He was mum's friend.

TEACHER: Right. And whose idea was it to do Speech and Drama?

CRYSTAL: Mum's. She said she earns good money teaching and wants to give me a good start.

Continued ▸

TEACHER: I see. Well, let's have something mummy would be proud of, shall we? Don't fold your arms darling. Smile and fling away those inhibitions.

CRYSTAL: O – for – a –

TEACHER: Open your arms sweetheart.

CRYSTAL: O – for – a –

TEACHER: Let yourself go!

CRYSTAL: O – for – a –

TEACHER: Louder, bigger!

CRYSTAL: O – for – a –

TEACHER: For goodness sake Crystal, put some oomph into it!

CRYSTAL: *(Brilliantly)*
O for a muse of fire, that would ascend
The brightest heaven of invention!
A kingdom for a stage, princes to act,
And monarchs to behold the swelling scene!

TEACHER: Crystal, darling, where did that come from? Why didn't you do it like that before?

CRYSTAL: You never said.

by Clifford Jury

Followers

This play was written in 1915 and was based on the story of Cranford *by Elisabeth Gaskell. Cranford is a rural market town facing the oncoming Industrial Revolution. Strong women in the town like gossip and romance, and most do not want their way of life to change. In this scene, Miss HELEN Masters has come to call on Miss Lucinda Baines. She is received by SUSAN, the maid, in Miss Baines' parlour.*

SUSAN: Miss Baines says, will you please take a seat, Miss Masters, and she'll be down in a minute.

HELEN: *(Not sitting)* Susan, go at once and tell your mistress I shall be seriously offended if she has gone upstairs to change her cap on my account.

SUSAN: *(Severely)* Miss Baines would not think of receiving a visitor without changing her cap, Miss Masters.

HELEN: I am not a visitor here, and, if I am, this is an early morning-call and –

SUSAN: *(Finally)* Miss Baines is changing her cap and there's an end of it. She won't be long.

HELEN: *(Defeated, sitting)* Oh, I am sorry, but this was my only opportunity of seeing her. I return to London this afternoon.

SUSAN: *(Awed)* By the train, miss?

HELEN: *(Smiling)* Yes.

SUSAN: You have more courage than I have.

HELEN: Tell me, Susan, your mistress keeps well?

SUSAN: She's well enough. Will worry herself, you know. Solomon has been a great disappointment to her.

Continued ▸

HELEN: Solomon? Who is Solomon?

SUSAN: Solomon is the cat. He had kittens, and the shock nearly sent Miss Baines to her bed.

HELEN: Oh, dear!

SUSAN: We still call her Solomon because she's used to it, but things will never be the same again. Miss Baines feels that Solomon has deceived her.

HELEN: And you, Susan?

SUSAN: Oh, I am quite well. Miss – *(pausing awkwardly, then)* – Miss Masters!

HELEN: Yes. Nothing wrong?

SUSAN: No, but – Miss Masters – you are the one the mistress listens to. She's – there is one thing that sorely troubles me, and, if you would speak a word for me, I'm sure –

HELEN: What is it, Susan?

SUSAN: Well, miss, when I came here ten years ago – straight from the charity school it was – Miss Baines said when she took me: "Now, Susan, no followers," she said, and I said: "No, mem, never." I passed my word when I was too young to know, and there's many wouldn't keep it on that account, but –

HELEN: Do you want followers, Susan?

SUSAN: No, miss, I don't. Not followers. One follower at a time's enough for any woman.

HELEN: You've somebody in mind?

SUSAN: I've seen James Brown look at me and I wouldn't say if it wasn't for my promise but that James –

HELEN: I see.

SUSAN: But I promised and I'm not the one to break my word, only when I try to put it to the mistress it's as if she saw it coming, and there's something in her eye that stops me asking. And it's not as if she never had a follower herself.

HELEN: *(Rising)* Susan!

SUSAN: *(Defending herself)* A body can't live ten years in Cranford without hearing that old story of Miss Baines and –

HELEN: Hush, Susan.

SUSAN: Well, it's true, and, what's more, he's back from India now. I've seen him.

HELEN: Mr Redfern is back?

SUSAN: You spoke his name, not I. Yes, he's back.

HELEN: When?

SUSAN: I only know I was carrying the basket yesterday while Miss Baines bought the grocery in Mr Wilson's shop, and there was a gentleman inside when we went in, buying matches to light his cheroot –

HELEN: A cheroot in Cranford High Street!

SUSAN: Yes, miss, and he raised his hat to Miss Baines, and she gave a jump and held my arm hard, and just said: "Mr Redfern" – gasping, like that – "Mr Redfern," and went on giving her orders as if nothing had happened. She's a brave woman, though I say it that's her own servant. And, if she had him once, why mayn't I have James Brown?

HELEN: I will see what I can do, Susan.

by Harold Brighouse

Cloud Busting

DAVEY, a boy with 'fizzy feet' who has a powerful imagination and starts dancing at odd moments, is being bullied at school by the other students, including SAM. Sam's mum, unaware of what has been going on, tells Sam that he should befriend Davey. In this scene, Sam has to walk to school with Davey. Out of sight of their parents, Sam starts bullying Davey again.

SAM: Dance for us, Fizz. Go on.

DAVEY: Get off me.

SAM: Don't tell me what to do.

DAVEY: Why not? I can say what I like.

SAM: Or I'll tell your mum you've been pushing me around.

DAVEY: Tell her what you like… She saw my black eye and my bruises.

SAM: Never said it was me though, did you? You're a coward, Davey. A big liar who said you'd fallen over when the bus came to a sudden stop. *(Laughs)* And she believed you. *(He grabs him closer)* I can make you do anything I like. Yeah?

DAVEY: And this time, I'll tell.

SAM: Tell who?

(DAVEY begins to get breathless…)

DAVEY: Anyone. My mum… Mr Mackie… Your mum…

SAM: You wouldn't do that.

DAVEY: If that's what it takes… You can't keep doing this, OK?

SAM: Says who?

DAVEY: What have I done, hey?

SAM: You got fizzy feet…

DAVEY: What have I done...?

SAM: You're weird. You don't have to do anything.

DAVEY: So when will you... understand?

SAM: Understand what, Fizz?

(DAVEY's growing ever more breathless)

DAVEY: You wouldn't do this... to your big mates... would you?

SAM: Do what, Davey?

DAVEY: No...

SAM: Are you scared of me, Davey?

DAVEY: Please stop...

SAM: So scared you can't even breathe?

DAVEY: No...

SAM: Sounds like it. Can't you breathe, Davey? What's up, can't you breathe?

(DAVEY pushes at him)

DAVEY: I said stop! Stop it now! Stop!

(SAM pauses)

SAM: Do not touch me. Davey, do not even touch me.

(DAVEY gasps for air. He gets his breath back, takes in big gulps of air)

DAVEY: One good reason. Come on...

SAM: Cos you are an idiot.

DAVEY: Sometimes, yeah. I'll give you that.

SAM: You're just an idiot.

DAVEY: You've said that already...

Continued ▸

(SAM's in his face)

SAM: A scruffy, dorky idiot with fizzy feet.

DAVEY: I know…

SAM: And I hate you, alright! Why can't you just be normal Davey…? Cos then maybe you wouldn't annoy me so much like you annoy me right now!

(He shoves DAVEY. But this time DAVEY retaliates. He pushes at SAM)

DAVEY: And you think you don't annoy me?

SAM: You what?

DAVEY: Think you're perfect, is that it? Think you're unbeatable?

SAM: Will you stop?

DAVEY: Do you, Sam?

SAM: Get off me now…

DAVEY: Cos… you're not! You're just nothing!

(He gives SAM a forceful shove. SAM stumbles more than he expected)

DAVEY: Sam! Watch out!

SAM: Help me…

DAVEY: Sam!

(A screech of brakes squealing to a stop. The beep of a horn. DAVEY grabs SAM's arm, before he can fall, drags him out of the way. They stumble back, both falling to the ground. SAM sits there, in a daze)

SAM: The car stopped where I would have been lying.

DAVEY: If I hadn't dragged him out of the way in time…

SAM: I would have been dead if it wasn't for… If it wasn't for…

DAVEY: I think he was just shocked. Cos he just sat there…

SAM: While all these people… Everyone asking if I was OK…

DAVEY: If he was hurt… That's all they wanted to know.

SAM: And middle of it all, the car sped off. Some bloke reckoned he got the number plate but it's not like I was hurt or anything.

by Malorie Blackman, adapted by Helen Blakeman

The Railway Children

PETER and his sisters BOBBIE and Phyllis have moved with their mother to a house near the railway while their father is away. Many of their adventures have to do with new friends and situations involving the trains. In this scene, the children see a landslide onto the tracks, when a train is expected on the line in the next half hour. They have only a few minutes to try to prevent a disaster.

PETER: Hush! Stop! What's that sound?

BOBBIE: It's a sort of rustling… whispering… Look! The tree over there!

PETER: It's moving!

BOBBIE: So are the others. It's like the woods in *Macbeth*.

PETER: They're falling down the cutting on to the line!

BOBBIE: Look what a great mound it's made!

PETER: And there is so much dust. *(With a sense of urgency)* Oh, Bobbie. The 11.29 down hasn't gone by yet. We must let them know at the station, or there'll be a most frightful accident.

BOBBIE: Let's run… *(She begins to run off)*

PETER: Come back! There's no time. It's two miles away and it's past eleven.

BOBBIE: Couldn't we climb up a telegraph post and do something to the wires. They do it in wars.

PETER: They only cut them, silly. And that doesn't do any good. If we only had something red, we could get down on the line and wave it.

BOBBIE: They'd only think it was just US as usual. We've waved so often before. *(Excitedly)* Peter! What about our flannel petticoats – Phyl's and mine! *(Lifting up her skirt)* Look! They're red. *(Wriggling out of her petticoat, and starting to rip it into strips)*

PETER: Come on Phyl, tear it into little bits, like Bobbie. You do it too.

BOBBIE: If we can't stop the train, there'll be a real live accident, with people killed.

PETER: *(Leaving the tearing to BOBBIE and Phyllis, and scrambling in the undergrowth)* Here are some twigs. If we make holes in the flags we can run the sticks through the holes.

(BOBBIE and PETER scramble down to the track to set two of the flags between piles of stones between the sleepers. They then scramble away from the track and wait in silence)

BOBBIE: It feels as if we've been standing here for hours and hours.

PETER: It's only a few minutes but it certainly seems a long time.

BOBBIE: No one will ever notice these silly little red flannel flags. The train won't care. It will go rushing by them and tear round the corner and go crashing into that awful mound. And everyone will be killed. Oh Peter, what else can we do?

PETER: I just don't know. I can't think of anything else. All we can do is wait here for the train and try to stop it. It's the only thing we can do to warn them. We just haven't time to run and alert anyone or go and get help... and there is no way that we can move the mound. It's much too big!

BOBBIE: It's the waiting that's the worst.

PETER: Do keep still, Phyl. *(To BOBBIE)* It's hard to keep Phyl from running off too.

BOBBIE: Sssh! Peter... Phyl... Keep quiet! Listen! I can hear the distant rumble and hum of the metals. Look, I can see a puff of white steam in the distance. It's far away along that stretch of line but it's coming.

PETER: Stand firm and wave like mad! When it gets to that big furze bush step back, but go on waving! Don't stand *on* the line, Bobbie! Don't worry about Phyl. I'll hold on to her.

Continued ▸

BOBBIE: They don't see us! They won't see us! It's all no good!

PETER: The train is shaking so much, it has loosened the stones where we've stuck our flags. They're falling down already. It's coming too quickly. That was a useless idea.

BOBBIE: Then I'll just have to hold them, won't I? *(Jumping forward, picking them up in her hands and starting to wave the flags)*

PETER: Bobbie, come back! The train's getting nearer. It's hurtling along. Keep off the line!

BOBBIE: It's no good.

PETER: Stand back!

BOBBIE: Not yet, not yet! *(Waving her two flags right over the line)* The front of the engine looks so enormous. Oh, stop, stop, stop!

PETER: Bobbie. No one will hear you. *(Grabbing hold of his younger sister, and pushing her to the ground)* Keep down Phyl. Hold on to me! *(In despair)* Bobbie!

(BOBBIE bravely continues waving the flags in front of the on-coming train. The train finally comes to a halt just in front of where BOBBIE is standing)

BOBBIE: Peter! It's stopped. It's stopped. The engine itself must have heard me. *(Crying out)* I can't stop waving the flags!

PETER: *(Dragging Phyllis with him down the bank, as the driver gets out of the train and comes towards them)* Sir! Sir! It's a landslide! Just around the corner. You wouldn't have seen it in time. The train would have been derailed.

BOBBIE: *(Finally collapsing on the ground)* We had to stop you!

by E Nesbit, adapted by LAMDA

Level 2 Acting

Grade 5 Solo

Titles in Level 2 Acting: Grade 5 Solo

Androcles and the Lion

The scene takes place in ancient Rome. Androcles, a recently converted Christian, and his wife MEGAERA are running away from persecution. Their route has taken them into the depths of a forest. Androcles is a small, thin, ridiculous little man who might be any age. His wife is rather handsome, pampered, well fed and in the prime of life. She has nothing to carry and has a stout stick to help her along. She does not share his beliefs and did not want to leave the comforts of city life. She is tired and exhausted by their journey and furious with her husband.

MEGAERA: *(Suddenly throwing down her stick)* I won't go another step. I don't believe a word of it. You are always threatening me with wild beasts to make me walk the very soul out of my body when I can hardly drag one foot before another. We haven't seen a single lion yet.

(Tearing the bundle from his back) You cruel beast, you don't care how tired I am, or what becomes of me. *(She throws the bundle on the ground)* Always thinking of yourself. Self! self! self! always yourself. *(She sits down on the bundle)* A man ought to think of his wife sometimes.

Aren't you happy with me? You ought to be ashamed of yourself but you're not: you glory in it. You glory in everything. In making me a slave, and making yourself a laughing-stock. It's not fair. You get me the name of being a shrew with your meek ways, always talking as if butter wouldn't melt in your mouth. And just because I look a big strong woman, and because I'm good-hearted and a bit hasty, and because you're always driving me to do things I'm sorry for afterwards, people say "Poor man: what a life his wife leads him!" Oh, if they only knew! And you think I don't know. But I do, I do, *(screaming)* I do. *(Pausing)* Then why don't you treat me properly and be a good husband to me? You can return to your duty, and come back to your home and your friends, and sacrifice to the gods

Continued ▸

as all respectable people do, instead of having us hunted out of house and home for being dirty, disreputable, blaspheming atheists. Don't you dare to compare me to common people. My father owned his own public-house; and sorrowful was the day for me when you first came drinking in our bar. I can forgive a man being addicted to drink: it's only natural; and I don't deny I like a drop myself sometimes. What I can't stand is your being addicted to Christianity. And what's worse again, your being addicted to animals. How is any woman to keep her house clean when you bring in every stray cat and lost cur and lame duck in the whole countryside? You took the bread out of my mouth to feed them: you know you did: don't attempt to deny it.

(Rising) Oh! I won't bear it another moment. You used to sit and talk to those dumb brute beasts for hours, when you hadn't a word for me. Well, if you're fonder of animals than of your own wife, you can live with them here in the jungle. I've had enough of them and enough of you. I'm going back. I'm going home. Serve you right if you are sent back to Rome and thrown to the lions! I wish them joy of you.

(Screaming) Are you going to get out of my way and let me go home? No! Then I'll make my way through the forest; and when I'm eaten by the wild beasts you'll know what a wife you've lost. *(She dashes into the jungle and nearly falls over the sleeping lion)* Oh! Oh! Andy! Andy! *(She totters back and collapses into the arms of Androcles, who, crushed by her weight, falls on his bundle)*

by George Bernard Shaw

The Terrible Fate of Humpty Dumpty

When a new boy, Terry, joins SAMMY's school, he is immediately bullied and intimidated by the gang leader Stubbs. Terry desperately wants to be accepted by the other boys and will do anything to please Stubbs. Although Sammy tries to befriend Terry, he keeps quiet when Stubbs expects Terry to complete a dangerous dare which eventually leads to his death. In this scene, after the terrible event, Sammy is trying to tell the police what actually happened.

SAMMY: I'm sorry… I tried to help but… I'm sorry…

(He faces the audience, and says)

… We killed him!

(The police officers move into the background)

It was an accident. Sort of. Nobody wanted it to happen. Except Stubbs, perhaps. I wouldn't put anything past Stubbs. He's mad, Stubbs is. Round the bend. It was him who started it all. Started having a go at Terry. I don't know why. He just decided he had it in for him. He'd only been at school for about a week. He was in my class. I'd spoken to him a few times. He seemed all right. A bit quiet, a bit shy. But he was all right. Then Stubbs decided to have it in for him. Nobody knows why. Nobody knows how Stubbs' mind works.

(A pause)

I'm trying to remember!…

(A pause. Then he continues)

… It was about a week after he started at school. We was in the playground talking together. And Stubbs and some of the others came up. I said, they're all right, really. Just having a joke. They like to have a joke. You'll get used to them. It's 'cos you're new. Once you've settled in they won't bother you no more…

Continued ▸

Terry didn't believe me. He knew they wouldn't leave him alone. I knew it, too. I could tell. Stubbs had it in for him from then on. And the others just followed Stubbs. Me too, I suppose. There was something about Terry. I don't know what it was. Something that made you want to have a go at him. He never stood up for himself. He just stood there and took it.

That's how it went. Every day. Week after week. Just getting on to him, making him bring money, waiting for him after school. They never beat him up or anything. They didn't need to. He did everything they said. I wish he'd have stood up to them just once. That would have been better than giving in all the time. Stubbs got to hate him more and more. Because he took it. He couldn't understand him, you see. He couldn't understand why he just took it all the time.

I know I should've done something. I should've told somebody, tried to get it stopped. They was my mates, though. You can't tell on your mates, can you?

(A pause. Then SAMMY says)

... It was Stubbs. He was the one. I was scared of Stubbs. Everybody was. It was like he was... I dunno... just bad... right the way through. He made everybody act like him. You couldn't help it. It was Stubbs.

I didn't tell anybody. *(A pause)* He stayed away from school. The whole of that week. They didn't seem bothered about it. They never even talked about him. It was like they'd forgotten all about him. I thought perhaps they had. So I decided to go round to his house and tell him that everything was all right again, and he could start coming back to school. I never got the chance. The day I was gonna do that, Terry's Dad came up to school. And Stubbs saw his Dad. That's when it all started again.

Stubbs told Terry he would have to take a little test. He wanted everybody to be at the waste ground after school.

(There is a pause)

I told him to go home. I said, go home, Terry. Don't wait round here. You've still got time. Are you round the bend? You know what's gonna happen, don't you? Stubbs is gonna get you. I heard Jimmy say. They're gonna get you.

I told him to go. Before it's too late. But it was too late. Pete threw the frisbee and it got stuck in the pylon. Stubbs made Terry climb up for it. They all made him, chanting "Humpty Dumpty" over and over and over again. I begged him to come down…

I'm sorry, Terry. I let you down. I tried, but it wasn't good enough. I'm sorry…

(A pause. Then SAMMY says)

Forgive me. Forgive us all.

(The lights fade slowly to black-out)

by David Calcutt

The Merchant of Venice

LAUNCELOT GOBBO is the young servant of Shylock, the moneylender. In this street scene, he is deciding whether to run away from his master. He is talking to the audience.

LAUNCELOT GOBBO:

Certainly, my conscience will serve me to run from this Jew my master: the fiend is at mine elbow, and tempts me, saying to me, "Gobbo, Launcelot Gobbo, good Launcelot," or "good Gobbo," or "good Launcelot Gobbo, use your legs, take the start, run away." My conscience says "No; take heed honest Launcelot, take heed honest Gobbo," or as aforesaid "honest Launcelot Gobbo, do not run, scorn running with thy heels." Well, the most courageous fiend bids me pack, "Fia!" says the fiend, "away!" says the fiend, "for the heavens rouse up a brave mind" says the fiend, "and run." Well, my conscience hanging about the neck of my heart, says very wisely to me: "My honest friend Launcelot" – being an honest man's son, or rather an honest woman's son, for indeed my father did something smack, something grow to; he had a kind of taste; – well, my conscience says "Launcelot budge not!" – "Budge!" says the fiend, – "Budge not!" says my conscience. "Conscience" say I, "you counsel well, – Fiend" say I, "you counsel well," – to be rul'd by my conscience, I should stay with the Jew my master, who (God bless the mark) is a kind of devil; and to run away from the Jew I should be ruled by the fiend, who (saving your reverence) is the devil himself: certainly the Jew is the very devil incarnation, and in my conscience, my conscience is but a kind of hard conscience, to offer to counsel me to stay with the Jew; the fiend gives the more friendly counsel: I will run fiend, my heels are at your commandment, I will run.

by William Shakespeare

Vicious Circle

This scene takes place in a twin-bedded room in a young offenders' detention centre. LAURA is a new inmate but Hollie has been here for months and has a reputation as a bully. Until now, Laura hasn't spoken to any of the inmates about why she has been detained. When Hollie asks about a photograph, pinned to the wall by Laura's bed, she reveals the chilling story of her crime.

LAURA: That's Amy. She was my best friend. The times we had together! You wouldn't believe some of the things we got up to… or maybe you would… I can trust you can't I?

Well, it happened last summer. I heard that Amy had been seeing my boyfriend David behind my back. I asked her if there was any truth in the rumours and she said "Yes." It was as though my feelings counted for nothing. You've no idea how hurtful that was. I didn't care about David – it wasn't serious – but that was no excuse for the deception. Every time we'd talked and laughed, like friends do, she'd been lying. A whole month of laughing and lying and laughing and lying. I just wanted to talk to her. I wanted her to see how hurt I'd been. One Sunday, when I knew that she'd be walking her dog down by the river, I waited for her on the bridge. There she was, carefree and happy in the sunshine. *I'd* lost weight. *I'd* shut myself away. I ran after her. Her pathetic little dog kept snapping at my heels. I wanted to kick it but I was trying so hard to be reasonable! Then she turned her back on me. Nobody does that.

(LAURA's mind is now on the riverbank, reliving the memory of what happened)

I watched her walk away. I ran at her with all the speed I had in me. I slammed my hands into her back and she screamed and fell forward, sprawled out on the footpath. She struck her head on the stone slab at the edge and went over into the water. She floated in a standing position. Her head just above the surface, her arms out to her sides, she was just staring. Then she gasped for air and her eyes came

Continued ▸

alive. She started screaming and thrashing about. Someone was going to hear the commotion so I moved to the edge of the path and placed my foot on top of her head. I pushed down smoothly and she sank. It took longer than I expected for the bubbles to stop coming from her mouth but when they did she was completely still. My leg ached. I lifted my foot and she stayed there, her hair spread out around her. I saw my reflection in the water…

(LAURA's mind is back in the room)

Someone saw it all from the bridge. Some stupid kid, who couldn't mind his own business. You may have noticed that I like to have things facing me. My little ornaments. See? Everything really. *(Looking at Amy's photograph and smiling)* Amy will always face me now.

(Turning to Hollie, her face suddenly fixed with a serious expression) You are going to be a friend aren't you? You'd never turn your back on me would you? Because if you can't be trusted, you'll remind me of Amy and, well… that wouldn't be good for *either* of us… would it?

by Nick Teed

Sherlock Holmes: The Boscombe Valley Mystery

The detective SHERLOCK HOLMES, his friend Dr Watson and Inspector Lestrade are investigating the mysterious death of a man, McCarthy, at Boscombe Valley in the English countryside. The man's son, young McCarthy, is accused of his father's murder. Here, Holmes is examining the scene of the crime.

SHERLOCK HOLMES: *(Running round, like a dog picking up a scent, then stopping)* What did you go in the pool for, Lestrade?... No, don't answer that. I have no time. That left foot of yours with its inward twist is all over the place. A mole could trace it. There it vanishes among the reeds. Oh, how simple it would all have been had I been here before they came like a herd of buffalo and trampled all over it.

(Pointing to the ground) Here is where the party with the lodge-keeper came, and they have covered all tracks for six or eight feet round the body. But here are three separate tracks of the same feet. *(Draws out a magnifying glass and lies down to have a better view, talking to himself)* These are young McCarthy's feet. Twice he was walking, and once he ran swiftly. The soles are deeply marked and the heels hardly visible. That bears out his story. He ran when he saw his father on the ground. Then here are the father's feet as he paced up and down. What is this, then? It is the butt-end of the gun as the son stood listening. And this? Ha, ha! What have we here? Tiptoes! Tiptoes! Square too, quite unusual boots! They come, they go, they come again. Of course, that was for the cloak. Now where did they come from?

(Runs up and down, sometimes losing, sometimes finding the track. Lies down on the ground and lets out a cry of satisfaction) Ha! *(Collects bits of evidence from the ground and then gets up)*

It has been a case of considerable interest. I fancy that this grey house on the right must be the lodge. I think that I will go in and have a word with the lodge-keeper. When I have done that, we

Continued ▸

may drive back to our lunch. You may walk to the cab, and I shall be with you presently. *(Handing something to Lestrade)* By the way, Lestrade, this may interest you. The murder was done with it. Although there are no marks on it, I know that it had only lain there for a few days. The grass was growing under it. It matches the injuries. There is no sign of any other weapon. … The murderer? He is a tall man. Left-handed. Limps with the right leg. Wears thick-soled boots and a grey cloak. Smokes Indian cigars. Uses a cigar-holder. Carries a blunt pen-knife in his pocket. There are several other indications, but these may be enough to aid us in our search. *(Pause)* I know you are sceptical, Lestrade. But you work your own method, and I shall work mine.

by Sir Arthur Conan Doyle, adapted by LAMDA

Hamlet

Hamlet, prince of Denmark, has professed his love to OPHELIA, the daughter of Polonius, the Lord Chamberlain. He has begun to show signs of mental instability, however, since the death of his father, his mother's remarriage and visitations from his father's ghost. In this scene, Ophelia is clearly frightened and has come to tell her father about Hamlet's strange behaviour.

OPHELIA:

O my lord, my lord, I have been so affrighted.
My lord, as I was sewing in my closet,
Lord Hamlet, with his doublet all unbrac'd,
No hat upon his head, his stockings foul'd,
Ungarter'd and down-gyved to his ankle,
Pale as his shirt, his knees knocking each other,
And with a look so piteous in purport
As if he had been loosed out of hell
To speak of horrors, he comes before me.

He took me by the wrist and held me hard.
Then goes he to the length of all his arm,
And with his other hand thus o'er his brow
He falls to such perusal of my face
As a would draw it. Long stay'd he so.
At last, a little shaking of mine arm,
And thrice his head thus waving up and down,
He rais'd a sigh so piteous and profound
As it did seem to shatter all his bulk
And end his being. That done, he lets me go,
And with his head over his shoulder turn'd
He seem'd to find his way without his eyes,
For out o' doors he went without their helps,
And to the last bended their light on me.

by William Shakespeare

Madame Doubtfire

Daniel Hillard has been divorced by his wife, and in order to see his children regularly he has been dressing up as Madame Doubtfire after answering an advertisement his former wife put in the local newspaper, hoping to find a child-minder. In this scene, LYDIA, his elder daughter, has come to see him after his disguise was discovered. Her father comes to the door of the flat to let her in.

LYDIA: Hullo Dad… I've come to see you… So *(she shrugs)* here I am. *(She is not happy. She walks into the flat and sits down)* No… I don't want any tea… you and Mum had such a barney, it was horrible. Horrible… you were both very nasty indeed… *(Confronting her father)* Listen, I don't want to talk, if you don't mind. Or listen, either. And I certainly don't want to talk about that… I'm only here because it's Tuesday… it's Tuesday tea-time. Which happens to be *your* time… *(She scowls)* It's just the principle of the thing… OK, so I'm asserting what is my right to see you… *(She sounds unhappy)* I'm not expecting to have a good time… OK, I'll have some tea. *(She takes her coat off and sits down. Her father gives her a mug of tea)* It isn't *just* the principle of the thing… there's something else as well. Something I thought about before a little, when Mum was telling us about your wedding. I thought then that, if either of you had backed out, none of us children would have ever been born… *(Trying to make her Dad understand)* Yes! And that's the point. We were born. And we're the only things that lasted aren't we? I mean, the marriage was a failure. A total failure. And you two aren't really even friends any more… *(She shakes her head, and then jumps up)* Oh! I know you make a pretty good show of getting along well when you bump into one another at other people's parties, or at school evenings and things like that. But you're not really good *friends* any more, are you? *(She sits closer to her Dad)* So, I was thinking, Natty and Christopher and me, we are the only three things to come out of that marriage. We're all that's left. We're the whole point now… Yes Dad! The whole point. The only reason you have any real contact. So that gives us a sort of extra right. Don't you see? Don't you see? If we three are not happy with the way things are, then what was the point of all those years? None! None at all! If you can't work things out to suit *us*, then it was all a total waste and a total failure. In fact... *(She hesitates, upset) Worse* than just total waste and failure, just hatred and arguments and all that ugly, ugly stuff... *(Angrily)* No, no, I didn't, I would have tried, but Mum wasn't listening. She was too angry and upset. *(She jumps up and goes to the window)* We had a fight. She didn't want me to come. She called me disloyal. She said you'd forfeited your right to a visit today. *(She is near to tears)* I told her I was not going to live my life between the two of you any more, thinking about her rights and yours. *(She is tearful, but confronts her Dad)* I told her I thought I had rights of my *own*, and from now on you two had better start thinking of *mine*... And I yelled it... I yelled at her that, if she didn't let me go today, she would regret it!

by Anne Fine, adapted by LAMDA

Confessions of a Shopaholic

REBECCA is a self-confessed shopaholic. She has agreed to meet her friend Jane in a café during her lunch hour. Jane is already at a table when she arrives.

REBECCA: Jane, I'm so sorry I'm late. They should list shopping under cardiovascular activity. My heart never beats as fast as it does when I see a 'reduced by 50 per cent' sign. *(Sitting down)* I count out the money in tens and twenties and wait, almost shivering as the shop assistant ducks behind the counter and produces the green box. She slides it into a thick glossy bag with dark green cord handles and hands it to me. I almost want to close my eyes, the feeling is so wonderful.

That moment. That instant when your fingers curl round the handles of a shiny, uncreased bag – and all the gorgeous new things inside it become yours. What's it like? It's like going hungry for days, then cramming your mouth full of warm buttered toast. It's like waking up and realising it's the weekend. Everything else is blocked out of your mind. It's pure, selfish pleasure. *(Turning to the waitress)* Oh, cappuccino please. *(To Jane)* Anyway, I walk slowly out of the shop, still in a haze of delight. I've got a Denny and George scarf. I've got a Denny and George scarf! I've got – then I heard him – "Rebecca." A man's voice interrupts my thoughts. I looked up and my stomach gave a lurch of horror. It was Luke Brandon. You know – Luke – the manager… Luke Brandon is standing on the street, right in front of me, and he's staring down at my carrier bag. I feel myself growing flustered. What's he doing here on the pavement anyway? Don't people like that have chauffeurs? Shouldn't he be whisking off to some vital reception or something?

"Did you get it all right?" he says, frowning slightly.

"What?"

"Your aunt's present."

"Oh yes," I say, and swallow. "Yes I… I got it."

"Is that it?" He gestures to the bag and I feel my cheeks flame red.

"Yes," I say eventually. "I thought a… a scarf would be nice."

"Very generous of you. Denny and George." He raises his eyebrows. "Your aunt must be a stylish lady."

"She is," I say, and clear my throat. "She's terribly creative and original."

"I'm sure she is," said Luke, and pauses. "What's her name?"

Oh God. I should have run as soon as I saw him, while I had a chance. Now I'm paralysed. I can't think of a single female name.

"Erm… Ermintrude," I hear myself saying.

"Aunt Ermintrude," said Luke thoughtfully. "Well, give her my best wishes."

He nods at me, and walks off, and I stare after him, trying to work out if he guessed or not. You see Jane, after all – I had asked him to have extra time to buy a present for my aunt! *(The waitress brings the cappuccino)* Thank you! I was ready for this.

by Sophie Kinsella, adapted by LAMDA

Wuthering Heights

In this scene, the young HEATHCLIFF has arrived back from an escapade on the moors, wet and alone. He is explaining to the kindly housekeeper, Nelly, what has happened.

HEATHCLIFF: Cathy is at Thrushcross Grange. I would have been there too, but they did not have the manners to ask me to stay. In fact, they threw me out because I laughed at them... and cursed a bit too!

Let me get this jacket off. I'm wet through.

(Taking his wet jacket off) It's a long story, Nelly. Cathy and I escaped from the washhouse and thought we would just go and see whether the Lintons passed their Sunday evenings standing shivering in corners! We ran from the top of the Heights to the park, without stopping. We crept through a broken hedge, groped our way up the path, and planted ourselves on a flower-plot under the drawing-room window. Both of us were able to look in by clinging to the ledge. It was exciting!

We saw a splendid place carpeted with crimson, and crimson-covered chairs and tables, and a pure white ceiling bordered by gold. There was a shower of glass-drops hanging in silver chains from the centre and shimmering with little soft tapers. Old Mr and Mrs Linton were not there; Edgar and his sisters had it entirely to themselves. We should have thought ourselves in heaven!

But you'll never believe what we saw next! Isabella lay screaming at the farther end of the room, shrieking as if witches were running red-hot needles into her. Edgar stood on the hearth weeping silently, and in the middle of the table sat a little dog, shaking its paw and yelping; which, from their mutual accusations, we understood they had nearly pulled in two between them. That was their pleasure! To quarrel over who should hold a heap of warm hair! Then, each began to cry because both, after struggling to get the dog, refused to take it.

We laughed outright – rather loudly too. The Lintons heard us, and with one accord they shot like arrows to the door. We made frightful noises to terrify them still more, and then we dropped off the ledge, because we felt we had better flee. I had Cathy by the hand, and was urging her on, when all at once she fell down. They had let the bulldog loose and it had seized her ankle! The dog was throttled off and a manservant took Cathy in his arms and carried her inside the house.

I followed, grumbling. When Isabella saw me she shrieked even more and said that I was a 'Frightful thing' and looked exactly like the son of the fortune-teller who had stolen her tame pheasant!

They said I was wicked – so I let them think I was and I started cursing again – so that Robert, the manservant, was ordered to send me away. That's why I am here and Cathy has remained behind.

(Softly) Don't be angry, Nelly.

by Emily Brontë, adapted by LAMDA

The Date

KARL is sitting in his bedroom. His laptop is placed in front of him. In this scene, he is speaking to his best friend, John, and trying to decide what he should do to unravel a mix-up he has created by trying to organise a date for his older sister, Melanie.

KARL: *(Looking at the computer)* How on earth can I get out of this? I can't believe what I have done? Fixed my sister up for a date with *Mr Lehman. Lehman* – our English teacher, I mean that is so... so... awful! He is *quite* young, I suppose, about thirty... and she's actually twenty-six – although her online profile said she was only twenty-two! But... urghhh... just the thought of it makes me feel sick... and it's all my fault!

(Moving towards the computer) It started out as a joke. I was so fed up with her moaning night after night that she was so lonely... so bored... and friendless since she moved back home. I said – well, why don't you make friends at work! That went down like a lead balloon! She works in a nursery! All the others are women and they're old enough to be her mother! Anyway – one of her old school friends said that she had met her boyfriend online... through this dating agency! That's when the fun began! You see, Mel created her profile. I read it. Well, it was sort of private, but I know her password... she doesn't know that... but I just worked it out. It was easy! She has this thing about a certain poet...Byron of all things... and an actor called Benedict! She even called her dog Byron and the cat Benedict! I don't always understand girls, do you? Anyway, I put the two names together and... Bingo! I could access her files!

(Turning the laptop on and accessing the site) Look! See how easy it is. *(Thoughtfully)* Perhaps I could become a hacker? I do seem to have a talent for this! *(Scanning Mel's profile)* Look, John. This sounds so much more interesting than her original description. Yes, well each person has to really make themselves sound irresistible to any boy – or, in her case – man – reading it! I kind of thought – I'll pretend that *I* am looking for a girlfriend and write a description of the sort of girl *I* would like to date! *(Moving away)* That was a

mistake. You see, she had written that she was a short, slim woman of twenty-two with short brown hair, brown eyes and a love of English Literature. She then went on to describe her Master's thesis on Byron! I mean – who is going to get excited about a very boring girl who likes Byron! I just altered it a *little*. I like tall, well-built blonde girls with blue eyes! So…I made her taller, bigger and blonder… Oh, and changed her eye colour too! I left the bit about Byron. I didn't feel I could change everything!

(Self-consciously) The next night, at supper, she was just so excited! "I've had a reply" she said, "someone wants to take me out! I didn't even know that I had posted it!" I couldn't tell her that I had! She went on to describe the man… his age… his interests… and, wait for it, his place of work! It was then that I knew exactly who he was! Lehman! *Mr Lehman*! They've arranged to meet up – go out for a meal! As if that wasn't bad enough… he'll think she tells lies! I mean… she doesn't look anything like the description I sent! What am I going to do?

by Anne Odden

Grade 5 Duologue

Titles in Level 2 Acting: Grade 5 Duologue

Victims

An unpopular slaughterman in a close-knit farming community has committed suicide after a public meeting has ruled that his business lease will not be renewed. A group of young protesters disrupted the meeting in an effort to sway the voting against him. The leader of the group was his own son JAMIE, whose aim was to force an inquiry into the methods used to kill the livestock. This scene takes place in the living room of Jamie's best friend LEWIS, the morning after the body was found.

JAMIE: I just… I feel as though my whole world's been turned upside down. I shan't sleep. I don't think I'll sleep for a long time. I'm sweating. I can feel it trickling down my back and it's cold. It's a cold morning.

LEWIS: You're only human Jamie. I can imagine how you must feel.

JAMIE: Can you? I don't think so. I don't think anybody can.

LEWIS: Give it time. You know what they say…

JAMIE: *(Standing)* Don't patronise me Lewis! Spare us both the embarrassment! Do you think you can make me feel any better by being so bloody understanding? So… calm and reassuring? I don't need your sympathy. Not yours, not anyone's.

LEWIS: I'm trying to help. Don't kick off with me because there's no one else around. What am I supposed to say? Tell me and I'll say it!

JAMIE: Don't say anything! You don't have to *say* anything. Just…

(There is a long pause as JAMIE softens. He stares into space, his mind racing)

JAMIE: I never thought they'd close him down. How could I be so…? *(He drops back onto his chair and holds his head in his hands. He is shaking)* We were happy, you know?

Continued ▸

LEWIS: I know.

JAMIE: We never argued over the small things. We never even disagreed about anything much. We were solid. I just took things too far.

LEWIS: Listen to me. Tell me to shut up if you want but I'm going to say this…

JAMIE: You don't have to…

LEWIS: Let me have my say! Stop blaming yourself and don't tell me that that's not what you're doing because I can read you like a book. I've known you for a long time Jamie and don't dare say that nobody understands because I do! You're blaming yourself for something your father did. He made that choice and you weren't there to stop him.

JAMIE: I should have been. I should have been there.

LEWIS: You said yourself, you didn't expect things to go that far. How could you have known what was going through his mind?

JAMIE: I should have seen the warning signs. He told me, just before the meeting… He said, don't do this son. Don't do it to your mother… He wasn't even thinking of himself. His eyes were pleading. I went into that meeting and I knew that if we jeered at him and shouted him down he'd lose the vote. He'd lose his livelihood, everything he'd worked for and I was there at the front shouting longest and loudest. So you tell me why I shouldn't take the blame, you tell me that.

LEWIS: You weren't there on your own. If you'd stayed out of it he'd still have lost the vote. Like it or not, there were more people in this community who disliked your father than liked him because of what he did for a living.

JAMIE: Every farming community's got slaughtermen!

(Pause)

LEWIS: All right, are you ready for the truth? It's not so much *what* he did but the *way he did it*! He drove round in his big four-wheel drive like he owned the land and everything on it!

He wasn't… *disliked* he was *hated*! He went about his work with a smirk on his face and he upset a lot of people. That meeting wasn't about getting rid of the slaughterhouse; it was about getting rid of your father! You thought you were all protesting about cattle prods and blood letting? Life goes on and in no time at all someone else'll be in that slaughterhouse carrying on where your father left off!

(The two stare at each other. What JAMIE knows to be the truth has stunned him into silence)

LEWIS: *(Calm but firm)* You're not saying I'm patronising now are you? So instead of sitting there wallowing in self pity you should be thinking of your mother and your sister…

JAMIE: *(Leaping to his feet, fists clenched, he is seething with rage)* He was my father! I'll…!

LEWIS: *(Standing to face him)* What? Come on Jamie! What are you going to do? Come on then; take it out on me if it'll make you feel better. I'm not going anywhere. Just don't expect me to lie down, I'll give as good as I get.

(Pause)

JAMIE: What a mess Lewis! I know what he was like and part of me hates him for what he's done to us but… *he was my dad... (He breaks down completely)*

LEWIS: *(Placing his hand on JAMIE's shoulder)* I know… I know…

by Nick Teed

Time

The main part of the scene takes place in the World War Two years. ROSE and LOUISA are best friends and at school together, where they make a pact. The scene opens some time in their future and then flashes back to the war years.

ROSE AND LOUISA: *(Together)* Time! We stand on the threshold of time. Once time was our friend. We never knew that time would be our enemy.

ROSE: *(Putting on the shawl and moving down stage left. She has aged considerably)* Where have the years gone?

LOUISA: *(Moving down stage right)* What would I have done with my years.

ROSE: Getting old! I didn't ask for this.

LOUISA: Would I have had silver hair when I got old?

ROSE: I miss my husband. Why did he have to leave me?

LOUISA: I would have liked to have known what it would have been like to be married.

ROSE: And my children – I never see them.

LOUISA: And children – I would have liked children.

(Pause)

ROSE: *(Turning to face diagonal stage right)* Louisa – it's not what we expected.

LOUISA: *(Turning to face diagonal stage left)* Rose! What is it like?

(Flashback. The girls move into the centre and pretend to be asleep. ROSE is now a young girl)

ROSE: Louisa! Louisa, are you awake? *(Propping herself on an elbow)*

LOUISA: Yes.

ROSE: Do you think the rest of the dorm is asleep?

LOUISA: I think so. Ruth is snoring her head off and Becky has just done her usual grunt.

ROSE: Only a few more weeks and we'll be free of this place. No more curfews and reporting. We'll be able to make our own decisions, go our own way.

LOUISA: Oh Rose – what is 'our own way'?

ROSE: I don't know. Who knows what the future holds. All I do know is that it has to be better than this.

LOUISA: Rose we will still be friends when we leave here, won't we? I couldn't bear it if I lost your friendship.

ROSE: I'm sticking to you like glue. Who would I have for my chief bridesmaid if you weren't around?

LOUISA: Really! Your chief bridesmaid?

ROSE: Of course! What a day that will be.

LOUISA: I know, we'll make it a double wedding.

ROSE: *(Stands)* With two dashing, handsome men by our sides.

LOUISA: *(Stands)* Both tall and slim with fire in their eyes.

ROSE: And their hearts and minds only for us. *(They hold hands)*

LOUISA: We'll honeymoon in Paris. *(Build pace)*

ROSE: And take an evening cruise along the Seine.

LOUISA: Visit the Eiffel Tower.

ROSE: Climb up to Notre Dame.

LOUISA: And seal our wedding vows – there in the cathedral.

ROSE: Together.

LOUISA: Together.

Continued ▸

ROSE: *(Turning round in excitement)* Oh! Louisa, we are going to have such a wonderful time.

LOUISA: *(Looking above the heads of the audience)* Children Rose – I want children – lots of them.

ROSE: *(Looking above the heads of the audience)* Two boys and two girls.

LOUISA: With blond curly hair.

ROSE: And shining eyes.

(They both look stage right as if hearing something)

LOUISA: Three o'clock. We must get some sleep.

ROSE: I know what we must do. Whenever we hear three chimes we must stop what we are doing and always think of each other and say the other's name. Promise me Louisa?

LOUISA: I promise.

(Both girls now stand centre with one shoulder touching and standing on a slight diagonal away from each other)

ROSE: We kept our promise.

LOUISA: For two years.

ROSE: Whenever we heard three bells we stopped what we were doing and said each other's name.

LOUISA: Until the day of the air-raid.

ROSE: I never could understand what happened that day. Why was Louisa standing outside the Town Hall when she knew the siren had gone? Why didn't she go down into the shelter?

LOUISA: Rose I kept my promise to the end. Perhaps if I had not waited for the Town Hall clock to strike three I would have made the shelter.

ROSE AND LOUISA: *(Move into the positions they had at the beginning. The following moves will be the same as the opening sequence)*

Time! We stand on the threshold of time. Once time was our friend. We never knew that time would be our enemy.

ROSE: *(Putting on the shawl)* Where have the years gone?

LOUISA: What would I have done with my years.

ROSE: Getting old! I didn't ask for this.

LOUISA: Would I have had silver hair when I got old?

ROSE: I miss my husband. Why did he have to leave me?

LOUISA: I would have liked to have known what it would have been like to be married.

ROSE: And my children – I never see them.

LOUISA: And children – I would have liked children.

(Both girls move to the centre and then look as if listening)

ROSE: Louisa – it's not what we expected. *(Drops to the floor)*

by Jenny Thornton

Blue Stockings

The play is set at Girton College, Cambridge, the country's first higher education college for women, in 1897. This year there will be a vote to decide whether the girls will be allowed to graduate officially, like their male counterparts, or whether – as has been the case up to this point – at the end of their course they will simply be sent home with a pat on the back. GERTIE is a student at Girton. Earlier in the week she met RALPH (a student at Trinity College) in the library. By means of a note, which he put inside a book, he arranged to meet her in the orchard.

(Girton's orchard. RALPH waits leaning against a tree. GERTIE appears from the kitchen. It's dark and very quiet. She creeps to one tree. He creeps to another. She moves in the shadows from tree to tree, becoming increasingly anxious)

GERTIE: Curses.

(He follows her. She stops under an apple tree. He creeps round the other side and puts his hand out to steady her)

RALPH: Evening.

(She screams)

Shhh!

GERTIE: Heavens!

RALPH: I'm so sorry if I scared you.

GERTIE: Dear Lord!

RALPH: I didn't mean to.

GERTIE: It's so dark, I was afraid.

RALPH: Me too.

GERTIE: You're not scared!

RALPH: I am. Thought your old chaperone might be on the prowl.

(She giggles)

RALPH: Listen, I'm sorry I asked you here. I've been paralysed with guilt.

GERTIE: It's alright.

RALPH: You mustn't get into trouble. It's the last thing I'd want.

GERTIE: No one saw.

RALPH: How did you get out?

GERTIE: I made an attempt through the window but it's rather treacherous in these. *(She indicates her skirts)*

RALPH: I'll say.

GERTIE: So I snook out through the kitchen.

RALPH: An adventuress. Come, sit down. There's a bench over here.

GERTIE: We can't be seen?

RALPH: I don't think so. Look, I don't even know your name.

GERTIE: Miss Moffat. Gertrude. My friends call me Gertie.

RALPH: Well, Miss Moffat, it's a pleasure to meet you.

GERTIE: You too, –

RALPH: Ralph Mayhew. 'Esquire'.

(They shake hands rather formally. A beat)

I'm sorry, I'm not very good at all this. I'm sure most fellows would ask a girl to a cosy tearoom. Or a clarinet concert, or something. Not to some spooky orchard.

GERTIE: It is a bit.

Continued ▸

RALPH: I know. *(Mimicking a ghost)* Woooo! Look, I hope you don't mind. I wrote you something. But please forgive me, it's not very accomplished. In fact, I have a horrible suspicion that it's dreadful.

GERTIE: I don't suppose so.

RALPH: It's a poem. But it's my first. Actually, perhaps I shouldn't –

GERTIE: No, please.

RALPH: It really is dire.

GERTIE: Go on.

(He looks at her. He takes a slip of paper out and reads painfully)

RALPH:
'My mistress' eyes illuminate my sleep,
Not only beauteous, she, but she is able.
Into a novel thoughtfully she does – peep,
Whilst I gaze longingly along the table.'

GERTIE: I don't know what to say.

RALPH: You don't have to say anything.

(A beat)

It's monstrous isn't it?

GERTIE: It's not that –

RALPH: It is, isn't it?

GERTIE: It's – terrible.

RALPH: I knew it.

GERTIE: I'm sorry!

RALPH: I'm afraid there's more. But I will spare you.

GERTIE: No please, I want to hear it.

RALPH: Only so you can jest.

GERTIE: Please.

RALPH: Promise not to laugh?

GERTIE: I promise.

RALPH: 'And as she gazes deeply with those eyes – '

(She gets the giggles)

GERTIE: I'm sorry, I'm sorry. Go on.

RALPH: I warned you!

'And as she gazes deeply with those eyes
I wish for one mere moment I could be
That leathern novel, object of her eye,
Which now she contemplates so tenderly.'

(She watches him carefully, and is moved. Pause)

GERTIE: That was quite beautiful.

RALPH: Now you're just humouring me.

GERTIE: Really.

RALPH: I'm not really a words man.

(Pause)

Miss Moffat, may I kiss your hand?

(GERTIE extends her hand. He takes it and kisses it politely. He holds onto it for just a second)

RALPH: You're getting cold. You mustn't stay out any longer.

GERTIE: Thank you for your unusual poem. I enjoyed it immensely.

RALPH: Literature was never my forte. I'm a scientist. Maybe next time I might show you an experiment.

GERTIE: I should like that. May I keep your poem?

RALPH: I can't think what you'd want to –

Continued ▸

GERTIE: Please.

RALPH: Alright. But, for the sake of Mr Wordsworth and his fellows, keep it under your hat. So to speak. Wouldn't like them getting wind of the competition.

GERTIE: I shall do just that.

(She loosens her hat and he places the poem on her head. She puts her hat back on. They look at each other for a moment)

RALPH: Until next time, good night Miss Moffat.

GERTIE: Good night.

(She goes in, he begins to walk away)

Wait! How will I know...?

RALPH: *(As he's leaving)* I'll leave you a note. A sign. Look out for it. Goodnight, sweet mistress!

GERTIE: Good night.

(She watches him go. A beat. She has a little moment of elation in the doorway before she runs back inside)

by Jessica Swale

A Midsummer Night's Dream

HERMIA runs into a wood near Athens to elope with Lysander against the wishes of her father who wants her to marry Demetrius. He, in turn, is loved by her friend HELENA. When Helena tells him of Hermia's plan, Demetrius also runs into the wood to find the lovers, closely followed by Helena. Oberon, the King of the Fairies, takes pity on Helena but his plan to help her goes wrong when Puck, his goblin, mistakenly puts a love potion on the eyes of Lysander and not Demetrius. This causes Lysander to profess his love for Helena. In this scene, at the height of the confusion, Hermia shows her distress for a situation which she cannot understand and Helena fights back.

HERMIA:
O me!
(To HELENA) You juggler! You canker-blossom!
You thief of love! What, have you come by night
And stol'n my love's heart from him?

HELENA:
Fine, i'faith!
Have you no modesty, no maiden shame,
No touch of bashfulness? What, will you tear
Impatient answers from my gentle tongue?
Fie, fie, you counterfeit! You puppet you!

HERMIA:
'Puppet'! Why, so? Ay, that way goes the game!
Now I perceive that she hath made compare
Between our statures; she hath urg'd her height;
And with her personage, her tall personage,
Her height, forsooth, she hath prevail'd with him.
And are you grown so high in his esteem
Because I am so dwarfish and so low?
How low am I, thou painted maypole? Speak:
How low am I? I am not yet so low
But that my nails can reach unto thine eyes.

Continued ▸

HELENA:
I pray you, though you mock me, gentlemen,
Let her not hurt me. I was never curst;
I have no gift at all in shrewishness;
I am a right maid for my cowardice;
Let her not strike me. You perhaps may think,
Because she is something lower than myself,
That I can match her.

HERMIA:
'Lower'? Hark, again!

HELENA:
Good Hermia, do not be so bitter with me.
I evermore did love you, Hermia,
Did ever keep your counsels, never wrong'd you,
Save that, in love unto Demetrius,
I told him of your stealth unto this wood.
He follow'd you; for love I follow'd him;
But he hath chid me hence, and threaten'd me
To strike me, spurn me, nay, to kill me too:
And now, so you will let me quiet go,
To Athens will I bear my folly back,
And follow you no further. Let me go:
You see how simple and how fond I am.

HERMIA:
Why, get you gone! Who is't that hinders you?

HELENA:
A foolish heart that I leave here behind.

HERMIA:
What! with Lysander?

HELENA:
With Demetrius. [...]
O, when she is angry, she is keen and shrewd;
She was a vixen when she went to school,
And though she be but little, she is fierce.

HERMIA:
'Little' again? Nothing but 'low' and 'little'?
Why will you suffer her to flout me thus?
Let me come to her! [...]
You, mistress, all this coil is long of you.
Nay, go not back.

HELENA:
I will not trust you, I,
Nor longer stay in your curst company.
Your hands than mine are quicker for a fray:
My legs are longer though, to run away. *(Exit)*

HERMIA:
I am amaz'd, and know not what to say. *(Exit)*

by William Shakespeare

Teen Angel

PEGGY is a teenage girl who has just died and arrived at the foot of the stairway to heaven, where she meets GABRIELLA, a spirit guide. Peggy cannot remember much about her past life. Gabriella tells her that, in order to earn her wings and enter heaven, she will need to go back on a mission to resolve some unfinished business.

GABRIELLA: I see you've arrived. I almost thought you weren't going to make it. Modern medicine certainly creates a lot of uncertainty in my work these days.

PEGGY: Where am I?

GABRIELLA: You're climbing the stairway to heaven.

PEGGY: You mean that…

GABRIELLA: You've crossed over…

PEGGY: I'm dead?

GABRIELLA: You could say that.

PEGGY: But what happened? I don't remember… anything.

GABRIELLA: Souls are made to forget the pain and sorrows of life, especially the end. It's better that way.

PEGGY: But I remember so little about my life. I remember that my name is Peggy and that I like vanilla ice cream… *(Pauses and struggles to remember. GABRIELLA comes down the stairs)*

GABRIELLA: Your memories are selected carefully. Too many earthly memories really mess with eternal bliss.

PEGGY: But it seems like I'm forgetting something. I hate that feeling. You know, like you know you have to do something but you can't remember what and you know you'll get in big trouble if you don't do it…

GABRIELLA: Peace, Peggy dear. There's nothing to worry about now.

PEGGY: I suppose not… *(Something still seems to bother her)*

GABRIELLA: *(Studying PEGGY)* I see what they mean…

PEGGY: What who mean?

GABRIELLA: I was sent to help guide you.

PEGGY: Guide me? Into heaven? *(Points to stairs)* The way looks pretty clear.

GABRIELLA: It appears so, but nothing is ever as simple as it seems. *(Motions to stairs)* Perhaps I should illustrate. Try going up the stairs.

PEGGY: *(Looks at GABRIELLA funny, shrugs, and heads to stairs. PEGGY stops at the bottom step and can't seem to go any further)* I want to… but can't.

GABRIELLA: You're not ready yet.

PEGGY: That doesn't mean that I'm going to… you know where…

GABRIELLA: *(Smiles)* Fortunately, no. You lived a good life and have few blotches on your record. You shouldn't fear going anywhere but heaven. But… *(Pauses)* … there's always a 'but' isn't there?

(PEGGY looks worried)

You will need to earn your wings.

PEGGY: Earn my wings?

GABRIELLA: You can't enter heaven without wings. So each soul must earn them. Now some people earn them in life with good works and good deeds… Mother Teresa for example. Her soul had the most amazing wings when she arrived…

Continued ▸

PEGGY: So I didn't do anything good in my life?

GABRIELLA: You were a good person or you wouldn't be here. But wingless souls are often wingless for a reason. Even good people make mistakes in life. So good people are given a chance to earn their wings despite problems in life.

PEGGY: Sounds fair. I only wish I knew what I'd done.

GABRIELLA: It's better not to know anything about your past life. It will only make earning your wings more difficult. Let me give you a warning… your memories are there, but don't go seeking them. They will only lead you down the wrong path and will keep you from earning your wings.

PEGGY: What happens if I don't earn my wings?

GABRIELLA: You will earn them. I know you will.

PEGGY: Why? Can you see the future?

GABRIELLA: No, but I can see your heart and I have faith that you will succeed.

PEGGY: *(Suddenly determined)* So what do I need to do to earn my wings?

GABRIELLA: There is some unfinished business in your past life that must be resolved. You will be without memory and will appear as a stranger to those who once knew you. Discover the problem and help to fix it. That will earn you your wings.

PEGGY: I have a feeling this isn't going to be as easy as you are making it sound.

GABRIELLA: Actually it is quite dangerous.

PEGGY: Then why send me?

GABRIELLA: Because we know that you are the only one that can fix the problem.

PEGGY: And what is the problem?

GABRIELLA: Unfortunately, we're not sure.

PEGGY: This isn't going to be easy.

GABRIELLA: I need to leave you with a warning as well.

PEGGY: Leave me? You're leaving me? But we just met.

GABRIELLA: Don't worry, Peggy. I won't be far away.

PEGGY: I feel so overwhelmed... no memory... trying to solve a problem I know nothing about... And you mentioned a warning?

GABRIELLA: You must be careful. Keep your memories buried. If one tries to seek the past, she can become trapped in it and become a lost soul.

PEGGY: A lost soul?

GABRIELLA: A lost soul is a person whom some people know as ghosts.

PEGGY: I could become a ghost?

GABRIELLA: *(Goes upstairs)* Only if you are not careful. Remember, you are someone else now. No one will remember you. No one will recognize you. But if they do... then you could be lost.

PEGGY: How will I know what to do?

GABRIELLA: You will know. Only you know the way. *(Reaches top of stairs)* Good luck, Peggy.

by D M Larson

The Player

This scene takes place in England in the 1590s. RALPH has run away from home. He has fallen in with a band of strolling players who have taken him in. HARRY is the young actor whose roles Ralph will be taking over. The scene is set in an inn yard.

HARRY: I hope you haven't got much stuff. There's not much room on the cart as it is, what with the costumes and the scenery.

RALPH: *(Showing him his bundle)* This is all there is. A spare shirt and a green leather belt that used to belong to my Uncle Walter.

HARRY: I hope you didn't steal it.

RALPH: I've never stolen anything in my life! Well, I took some bread and a hambone when I left my father's house. But that would have been mine to eat anyway so it doesn't really count as stealing, does it?

HARRY: A hambone, eh? Got any left?

RALPH: I finished it on Monday.

HARRY: *(Disappointed)* Oh. Was that your last proper meal?

(RALPH nods)

Well, at least you're used to going hungry.

RALPH: What do you mean? Master Honeybourne said players dined like kings.

HARRY: Did he promise you a feast?

RALPH: Roast swan and oyster pie with dish of frumenty to follow.

HARRY: Zachary Honeybourne is a fine leader of our troupe and an actor beyond compare – at least that's what he tells us – but he has been known to… how shall I put it? Exaggerate. For effect.

RALPH: You mean there'll be no feast?

HARRY: Don't worry, supper tonight will be worth the waiting. We had a good crowd in this afternoon and nobody escapes when I take the hat round. But it's not always like that.

RALPH: Really? Everyone likes plays, don't they?

HARRY: You'd be surprised. I've come across some right old miseries. Sometimes I think you have to be a misery to be a Justice.

RALPH: I don't understand.

HARRY: In every town we stop in, before we can do a play, we have to get a licence from the Justice of the Peace. Sometimes they refuse, or they're away or... Look, we do well enough. But make no mistake, there will be nights we sleep under the stars and have to tighten our belts.

RALPH: I don't mind. It'll be better than being at home.

HARRY: Good, then. As long as you know. Now, how's your juggling?

RALPH: I can't juggle.

HARRY: I thought as much. You'll pick it up soon enough. Can you play any instruments?

RALPH: I can bang a drum or rattle a tambourine.

HARRY: Anyone can do that.

RALPH: I can sing.
Hey nonny nonny,
Hey nonny hey...

HARRY: Yes, thank you, that's quite enough of that. How about curtseying? Any skill in that direction?

RALPH: I've never tried. Why would I?

HARRY: You'll be playing girls, why else? Village maidens, princesses, fairy queens, that kind of thing.

Continued ▸

RALPH: Girls?

HARRY: Mmm. Girls seem to curtsey a lot. In plays, anyway. Princesses specially, they're always at it. I think it's because Princesses wear the crimson farthingale and curtseying shows off the underskirt. The material cost more than a shilling a yard, Zachary's very proud of it. We'd better practise if you're going to play tomorrow.

RALPH: Tomorrow?

HARRY: You're going to be the Princess of Byzantium. Didn't Zachary say?

RALPH: Tomorrow? But I… I can't. I don't know what to do.

HARRY: Don't worry. It's only one line. 'My loving lord.' Have a go.

RALPH: 'My loving lord.' *(Trying some variations)* 'My *loving* lord.' 'My loving *lord*.' '*My* loving lord.'

HARRY: The first one. No, actually, the second. I never did it like that but it sounds quite good. And keep your voice high, remember, you're a girl.

RALPH: *(Squeaky)* 'My loving lord.'

HARRY: No need to squeak like a screech owl. Now, drop a curtsey. Like this.

(He drops a deep curtsey)

RALPH: Oh that's magnificent.

HARRY: Piece of cake. One foot behind, weight on the front leg, bend at the knee. Go on, you try.

(RALPH tries. It's rather wobbly)

Don't lean forward. Keep your back straight.

(RALPH tries again and almost falls)

Smoothly, smoothly.

(RALPH tries again. It's all going well – but then he loses his balance. HARRY catches his shoulders before he falls. RALPH cries out in pain)

RALPH: Ah!

(He pulls away from HARRY)

HARRY: What on earth is the matter?

RALPH: Nothing. Nothing at all, it's alright. Really.

HARRY: Is your shoulder hurt?

RALPH: It's nothing, I swear. Let's keep rehearsing, shall we?

HARRY: Let me see.

RALPH: No. Leave me alone.

HARRY: Ralph!

(A moment. RALPH concedes and allows HARRY to investigate his shoulder)

Who did this to you?

RALPH: My father. I don't want to talk about it.

HARRY: What had you done?

RALPH: It doesn't matter.

HARRY: Is this why you ran away from home?

(RALPH nods. For a moment we think HARRY will pursue the subject. Then...)

HARRY: It's alright. The Princess wears a ruff so the bruise won't show. We should find the others, it must be nearly dinner time. Race you there.

(He runs off. A moment. RALPH rubs his shoulder, then follows)

by Shaun McKenna

The Midwich Cuckoos

After a day when everyone in the quiet English village of Midwich mysteriously falls asleep, most women of child-bearing age in the village are found to be pregnant. They give birth to children who mature incredibly fast, have telepathic abilities, and can even control other people. When a mob of frightened and angry villagers tries to burn down the house where the Children live, the Children make them attack each other. In this scene, the Chief Constable SIR JOHN interviews one of the Children, ERIC. Although younger, Eric has the maturity and appearance of an older teenager.

SIR JOHN: This was a serious business last night. It is our job to clear it up and find out what really happened. Who was responsible for the trouble, and so forth. People keep on telling me that you and the others here were. Now, what do you say to that?

ERIC: *(Promptly)* No.

SIR JOHN: *(Nodding)* What happened, exactly?

ERIC: The village people came here to burn The Grange down.

SIR JOHN: You're sure of that?

ERIC: It was what they said, and there was no other reason to bring them here at that time.

SIR JOHN: All right. We'll not go into the whys and wherefores just now. Let's take it from there. You say some of them came intending to burn the place. Then I suppose others came to stop them doing it, and the fighting started?

ERIC: *(A little uncertainly)* Yes.

SIR JOHN: Then, in point of fact, you and your friends had nothing to do with it. You were just spectators?

ERIC: No. We had to defend ourselves. It was necessary, or they would have burnt the house.

SIR JOHN: You mean you called out to some of them to stop the rest, something like that?

ERIC: *(Patiently)* No. We made them fight one another. We could simply have sent them away, but if we had they would very likely have come back some other time. Now they will not. They understand it is better for them to leave us alone.

SIR JOHN: *(Puzzled)* You say you 'made' them fight one another. How did you do that?

ERIC: It is too difficult to explain. I don't think you could understand.

SIR JOHN: *(Irritated, but showing restraint)* Nevertheless, I'd like to hear.

ERIC: *(As one stating a fact)* It wouldn't be any use.

(Pause)

SIR JOHN: *(With growing irritation)* However it was done – and we'll have to go into that later – you are admitting that you were responsible for what happened?

ERIC: We are responsible for defending ourselves.

SIR JOHN: To the extent of four lives and thirteen serious injuries. When you *could*, you say, have simply sent them away.

ERIC: *(Indifferently)* They wanted to kill us.

SIR JOHN: I don't understand *how* you can have done it, but I take your word for it that you did, for the present. Also your word that it was unnecessary.

ERIC: They would have come again. It would have been necessary then.

SIR JOHN: You can't be sure of that. Your whole attitude is monstrous! Don't you feel any pity for these unfortunate people?

ERIC: No. Why should we? Yesterday afternoon one of them shot one of us. Now we must protect ourselves.

Continued ▸

SIR JOHN: But not by private vengeance. The law is for your protection, and for everyone's –

ERIC: The law did not protect Wilfred from being shot. It would not have protected us last night. The law punishes the criminal *after* he has been successful. It is no use to us. We intend to stay alive.

SIR JOHN: But you don't mind being responsible, so you tell me, for the deaths of other people.

ERIC: Do we have to go round in circles? I have answered your questions because we thought it better that you should understand the situation. As you apparently have not grasped it, I will put it more plainly. It is that if there is any attempt to interfere with us, by anybody, we shall defend ourselves. We have shown that we can. We hope that will be warning enough to prevent further trouble.

SIR JOHN: *(Furious)* You damned young blackguard! You insufferable little prig! How dare you speak to me like that! Do you understand who I represent? If you don't, it's time you learnt it, and I'll see that you do. So you're not to be 'interfered with', you'll defend yourselves, will you! Where do you think you are? You've got a lot to learn – *(Breaking off suddenly, he stares at ERIC and goes rigid. His eyes widen and he starts to whimper with fear, covering his face. He falls to the ground and claws at it, crying out)*

ERIC: *(To the others in the room)* He is not hurt. He wanted to frighten us, so we have shown him what it means to be frightened. He'll understand better now. He will be all right when his glands are in balance. *(Exits the room)*

by John Wyndham, adapted by LAMDA

Fragile Land

This play explores the difficulties of life for a new generation of young Londoners when they are pressured by the traditions upheld by their parents, who grew up in a different culture. In this scene, HASSAN, a young Afghan who fears deportation, expresses his wish to marry 17-year-old TASLEEMA.

(TASLEEMA enters)

HASSAN: Are you ready? *(TASLEEMA looks away)* I've been rehearsing my speech to your father all night. Look… *(He produces a piece of crumpled paper)* I have it all written – in Pashtun – because I can only speak from my heart in my own language. How was your father's mood this morning?

TASLEEMA: Hassan…

HASSAN: As soon as he gives his blessing, we must make arrangements. We should have a big party – yes? Invite all our friends…

TASLEEMA: You can't ask my father.

HASSAN: It doesn't matter if he says 'no' but we must do things properly. We will go ahead anyway. My father is eagerly waiting to meet you. *(HASSAN tries to kiss TASLEEMA but she turns away)* Are you okay?

TASLEEMA: No. Hassan. It's ridiculous. I can't marry.

HASSAN: But we've been through all this. It's for the best… for you…

TASLEEMA: No. I'm too young. I need to finish my school.

HASSAN: You are nervous – yes? I understand, it's a big step. But I want you to be comfortable. Not to be humiliated by the community.

Continued ▸

TASLEEMA: No.

HASSAN: Are you afraid of your father? I can work on him. He will listen to me. Sometimes, man to man is good.

TASLEEMA: This isn't about Abba. It's my decision. I can't marry you. Thank you for offering to help me though. It was very sweet.

(She turns to go)

HASSAN: Tasleema! Explain to me. What is happening?

TASLEEMA: I told you.

HASSAN: No. You can't change your mind just like that.

TASLEEMA: Yes I can. You don't love me, Hassan. You're only after one thing.

HASSAN: What are you saying?

TASLEEMA: I know you're being deported. I know you're desperate to stay in the country – but I can't just be your passport.

HASSAN: Who told you this? *(TASLEEMA is silent)* It is true. I am being thrown out of the country but that's not the only reason. I want to be with you.

TASLEEMA: And what about the four other girls you tried to marry?

HASSAN: What other four girls?

TASLEEMA: Don't lie to me, Hassan. I know!

HASSAN: We must marry. For both our sakes. *(TASLEEMA is silent)* I have a chance here, in this country, to be someone, to make something of my life. I want to work, I don't want to beg from this country. I want to contribute in some small way. You are like a small miracle to me. You can help me rebuild my life.

TASLEEMA: And what about my life?

HASSAN: We would be happy together... please... *(TASLEEMA is torn)* I would help in any way I can to get you through school. I want to help you. I don't want to go back. I have made a life for myself here, made friends, made plans – so many dreams.

TASLEEMA: And I have dreams too. I want to get some qualifications, have choices, decide for myself…

HASSAN: Let me speak to your father.

TASLEEMA: Hassan… listen to me.

HASSAN: Look me in the eye and tell me you would throw me back to the wolves. I have travelled long distances – you can be my shelter. I saw so many people killed. My mother was killed. She was dragged from our house because she was teaching girls secretly in our house.

TASLEEMA: I'm sorry…

HASSAN: They executed her, shot her in the street and I wasn't even there! They imprisoned me, beat me and my father and then threw us back out into the streets. We escaped over the border, I had to hide under sacks of salt over to Pakistan. I can't go back there.

TASLEEMA: It's not fair. You can't expect me to give up everything.

HASSAN: What would you be giving up? It is an exchange. I am offering you a new life!

TASLEEMA: It's not the life I want though. I don't want to be tied down at my age. My life's only really begun.

HASSAN: And if you refuse me, my life will end.

TASLEEMA: No. It won't, Hassan.

HASSAN: My mother was killed. I can't go back. I still have nightmares. She comes back to me when I am sleeping and she reaches for me but I cannot get to her.

TASLEEMA: What do you expect from me?

HASSAN: Our marriage will heal my wounds.

(Beat)

Continued ▸

TASLEEMA: I can't do it. *(HASSAN is stunned)* I can't go through with it. Maybe a few years down the road, another place, perhaps we could have a chance. But I have to do this for myself.

HASSAN: Where will you go?

TASLEEMA: I'm leaving home. Gonna try and make it on my own.

HASSAN: Where though?

TASLEEMA: I don't know yet.

HASSAN: What about me?

TASLEEMA: I'm sorry. We would have been doing it for all the wrong reasons.

HASSAN: My life is not reason enough?

TASLEEMA: I don't trust you. I look at you and I am filled with love and longing and hope and then I hear you've been trying to get married ever since you got here.

HASSAN: I am desperate to stay here. How can you blame me?

TASLEEMA: I don't. But you lied to me.

HASSAN: And if I had told you my real situation?

TASLEEMA: If you'd been straight from the start… maybe… but this way, I'll never know.

HASSAN: You won't survive five minutes on your own. You'll end up wandering the streets like all those shattered people out there. There is evil in this city. How will you cope?

TASLEEMA: I'll manage. I'm sorry I couldn't help you. I wish you all the luck in the world.

by Tanika Gupta

A Matchmaker Caught Off-Guard

EMMA Woodhouse is proud of her skill as a matchmaker. But a single success, as she considers, in that direction, leads her into a series of subsequent errors. She takes in hand the romantic interests of her friend HARRIET. First, she mismatches Harriet with Mr Elton, but Mr Elton shows that he doesn't care for her; then she encourages what she thinks is Harriet's interest in Mr Churchill, but Mr Churchill is also uninterested. Finally, and ironically, Harriet herself drops a bombshell which wakens Emma, for the first time, to the true object of her own inclinations.

HARRIET: Miss Woodhouse – if you are at leisure, I have something that I should like to tell you, a sort of confession to make!

EMMA: You look quite serious, Harriet – I beg you to speak!

HARRIET: I am an altered creature, *in one respect*, and it is fit that you should have the satisfaction of knowing it. I am too much ashamed of having given way as I have done. I dare say you understand me?

EMMA: Yes, I hope I do.

HARRIET: It seems like a madness! I can see nothing at all extraordinary in Mr Elton now. I do not care whether I meet him or not, indeed I would go any distance round to avoid him. I am now going to destroy what I should have destroyed long ago. Cannot you guess what this box holds?

EMMA: Not the least in the world. Did Mr Elton ever give you anything?

HARRIET: I cannot call them gifts, but they are things I have valued very much. *(She places her box on the table, opens it and holds up what she removes)*

EMMA: A small piece of – *court plaster*?

Continued ▸

HARRIET: Now, you *must* recollect!

EMMA: No, indeed. I do not.

HARRIET: Dear me! I should not have thought it possible you could forget what passed in this very room about court plaster. Do you remember Mr Elton cutting his finger with your new penknife, and your recommending court plaster? And as you had none about you, and knew I had, you told me to take mine out and cut him a piece? And it was too large, and he cut it smaller? And he kept playing some time with what was left before he gave it back to me? In my nonsense I put it by; I could not help making a treasure of it.

EMMA: My dearest Harriet, you make me more ashamed of myself than I can bear! Yes, I remember it all now. Oh, my sins, my sins! And I had plenty of plaster all the while in my pocket. One of my senseless tricks – to recommend you to each other. I deserve to be under a continual blush all the rest of my life.

HARRIET: I am sure I never suspected you had some at hand yourself, you did it so naturally.

EMMA: And you actually treasured this piece of plaster for his sake?

HARRIET: But here, here is something still more valuable – I mean that *has been* more valuable. Because this is what really did once belong to him, which the court plaster never did!

EMMA: The end of an old pencil?

HARRIET: This was really his! One morning, perhaps you do not remember, he wanted to make a memorandum in his pocket book, and this was left upon the table as good for nothing. But I kept my eye on it, and as soon as I dared I caught it up!

EMMA: I do remember it; I perfectly remember it. But go on.

HARRIET: Oh, that's all. I have nothing more to show you – except that I am now going to throw them both on the fire, and I wish you to see me do it.

EMMA: My poor dear Harriet! And have you actually found happiness in treasuring up these things?

HARRIET: Yes, simpleton as I was. I am quite ashamed of it now.

EMMA: But, Harriet, is it necessary to burn the court plaster? It might yet be useful.

HARRIET: It has a disagreeable look to me. There it goes, and there is an end, thank heaven, of Mr Elton!

EMMA: Well, Harriet, whenever you marry...

HARRIET: I shall never marry.

EMMA: Never marry! This is a new resolution. I hope it is not in compliment to Mr Elton.

HARRIET: No – to one so superior to Mr Elton!

EMMA: Ah, yes! There was a not very distant time when you gave me to understand so much. So you *do* care for Mr Frank Churchill?

HARRIET: Him! Never! How could you so mistake me?

EMMA: But, surely, when the service he rendered you in protecting you from the gipsies was spoke of...? You even mentioned what your sensations had been when you saw him come forward to your rescue.

HARRIET: But I was speaking of something very different! It was not the gipsies – not Mr Churchill. I was thinking of – of Mr Knightley, of his coming and asking me to dance, when Mr Elton so rudely refused to stand up with me.

EMMA: Mr Knightley?

HARRIET: That was the service which made me begin to feel... how superior he was to every other being upon earth!

EMMA: Mr Knightley! Good God! This has been a most unfortunate – most deplorable mistake!

by Jane Austen, adapted by Maureen Blythe
from Emma

Slob School

AMANDA is the proud owner of the Amanda Whinthrope School of Manners and Social Graces for the Hopelessly Slobby. Her new assistant, CHARLES, has benefited from her instruction and is now supposed to be a reformed slob. However, Charles is not very comfortable with being a 'gentleman'. In this scene, Amanda questions Charles about manners and social situations, much to his discomfort.

CHARLES: So you really believe that there is no such thing as a true, genetically predetermined slob, Ms Whinthrope? Born slobs, so to speak?

AMANDA: Yes, that is correct, Charles. Slobs are not born. They are made.

CHARLES: You mean they get it from their parents?

AMANDA: You can't just fault the parents, Charles. It's the whole environment. Society in general. Manners, etiquette, it's all gone to pot! And I, Amanda Whinthrope, owner and operator of the Amanda Whinthrope School of Manners and Social Graces for the Hopelessly Slobby, firmly believe that one can just as easily be taught to be a well-mannered, *bon vivant* as he or she can so easily degenerate into a socially unacceptable slob.

CHARLES: I hope you're right.

AMANDA: Charles, if you don't believe I can change a slob into a prince or princess, what do you think I turned you into and why do you choose to work here?

CHARLES: Well, the grease monkey job down at Sloppy Joe's Luborama was taken. So, heck, I said, I'll give slob school a shot, and here I am.

AMANDA: I hate when people call my establishment slob school! It's so uncouth!

CHARLES: When I was a slob, that's what I called this place.

AMANDA: Yes, but fortunately, you've changed.

CHARLES: You really think so?

AMANDA: Oh, yes. Just look at you. *(She does)* There you are, a former oily, grease-stained slob completely transformed into the epitome of style and grace.

CHARLES: *(Itchy, and uncomfortable in his tux)* Yeah, that's me. A real gent.

AMANDA: Now, you remember how I taught you to eat?

CHARLES: Yes.

AMANDA: Then let's sit at the table and practice. *(CHARLES sits as AMANDA paces about)* Are you comfortable?

CHARLES: *(Squirming and slouching)* Yeah, sort of.

AMANDA: Good, then stop squirming and sit up straight! *(CHARLES does)* Excellent. Now, remember what I told you to never ever do when eating?

CHARLES: Er... Oh, yeah. Never ever use my hands to eat. Use my spoon and fork at all times, especially when eating soup.

AMANDA: Good. Correct. But what else, Chuck?

CHARLES: Errr. Let's see... *(Thinks, picks up napkin)* Don't blow my nose in my napkin?

AMANDA: That's not what I was thinking of, but still I absolutely forbid you to ever do that! These are my best silk napkins!

CHARLES: No nose blowing! *(As AMANDA paces like a drill sergeant)* OK, so that wasn't it. So what else is there?

AMANDA: I'll give you a hint.

CHARLES: Great. I love hints.

AMANDA: Good. When eating soup, what don't we ever do?

Continued ▸

CHARLES: *(Thinks, scratches his head)* Ummm – make jokes about flies doing the backstroke in it?

AMANDA: No! No! Think!

CHARLES: *(Squeezes his eyes shut and strains to think)* Ummm, we... we... er – *(Opens his eyes and points at her)* Oh, I know!

AMANDA: What?!

CHARLES: We never slurp it!

AMANDA: Right! We never ever slurp our soup! Only uncouth slobs slurp their soup. Well-mannered persons *(waiting for CHARLES to answer)* simply... simply, Chuck, what do well-mannered persons do when eating soup?!

CHARLES: Stick the spoon in their mouth, shut their mouth, pull out the spoon and... and...

AMANDA: *(Slaps him on the back)* Swallow!

CHARLES: *(Choking, then)* R-right! *(Trying to catch his breath)*

AMANDA: Yes. Breathe, Chuck.

CHARLES: Right. Breathe. *(He catches his breath)* Breathe.

AMANDA: Yes. Now you see? I told you I could transform you into a gentleman.

CHARLES: It's amazing, Amanda. Do you think all the girls will like me now?

AMANDA: Did they like you before, Chuck?

CHARLES: No. They said I was an oily slime.

AMANDA: It must have been all that grease and oil from the Luborama they were referring to.

CHARLES: I don't know.

AMANDA: *(Thinks about it. Checks her watch)* Up, Chuck!

CHARLES: *(Shocked at the pun)* Now?! At the table?

AMANDA: Yes.

CHARLES: You sure?

AMANDA: Yes! Now! Up, Chuck!

CHARLES: OK, but I didn't think it was polite to do that at dinner table. But if you insist.

AMANDA: I insist! Up, Chuck!

CHARLES: You got it, but I'd stand back if I were you. *(He starts to stick his finger in his mouth and to gag)*

AMANDA: *(Horrified)* What are you doing?!

CHARLES: You told me to up chuck.

AMANDA: *(Pulls him up)* I meant for you to get up, Charles!

CHARLES: *(He jumps up)* Ohhh! *(Doorbell)*

AMANDA: Our first student. *(Hops around)* I'm so excited.

by Robert Mauro

Author Index

Acknowledgements

Rights in the pieces are strictly reserved and application for public performance must be made to the rights holders as listed below. For permission to reprint the copyright material in this anthology we make grateful acknowledgment to the following authors, publishers and executors:

Austen, Jane *A Matchmaker Caught Off-Guard* Adapted by Maureen Blythe from *Emma*. Used by permission of Samuel French Ltd **Ayckbourn, Alan** *Ernie's Incredible Illucinations* by Alan Ayckbourn. Published and used by permission of Faber and Faber Ltd **Aykroyd, Clarissa** *Running* Used by permission of Clarissa Aykroyd **Baum, L Frank** *The Wizard of Oz* Excerpt adapted from *The Wizard of Oz* granted courtesy of Warner Bros Entertainment Inc. All Rights Reserved, © 1939 **Bhuchar, Sudha** *Child of the Divide* © Sudha Bhuchar 2006, published by Methuen Drama, an imprint of Bloomsbury Publishing PLC **Blackman, Malorie** *Cloud Busting* Reproduced by permission of The Agency (London) Ltd. © Helen Blakeman 2011. All rights reserved and enquiries to The Agency (London) Ltd, 24 Pottery Lane, London W11 4LZ, fax 0207 727 9037 **Brazil, Angela** *A Terrible Tomboy* Adapted by LAMDA. Used by permission of IndependentAge **Brighouse, Harold** *Followers* Used by permission of Samuel French Ltd **Calcutt, David** *Beowulf* Reproduced with the permission of Nelson Thornes Ltd from Dramascripts Beowulf, David Calcutt, 9780174326564, first published in 2001. *The Terrible Fate of Humpty Dumpty* Reproduced with the permission of Nelson Thornes Ltd from Dramascripts The Terrible Fate of Humpty Dumpty, David Calcutt, 9781408519967, first published in 1998 **Cartwright, Ann** *Crush* From *Forty Short Plays*. Copyright © Ann Cartwright, 2000. Used by permission of Pearson Education Limited **Dahl, Roald** *The Twits* by Roald Dahl, adapted by LAMDA. Published by Puffin. Used by permission of David Higham Associates **Dickens, Charles** *The Haunting of Ebenezer Scrooge* Adapted by Maureen Blythe from *A Christmas Carol*. Used by permission of Samuel French Ltd **Edwards, Monica** *Dolphin Summer* Adapted by LAMDA, © The Monica Edwards Estate, used by permission of Girls Gone By Publishers **Emery, Jacqueline** *Extinct*, *The Maze*, *Stowaways* and *The Train* Used by permission of Jacqueline Emery **Farr, David** *Ruckus in the Garden* Used by permission of Curtis Brown Group **Fine, Anne** *Madame Doubtfire* by Anne Fine, adapted by LAMDA. Published by Puffin. Used by permission of David Higham Associates and Penguin Books Ltd **Gaiman, Neil** *The Graveyard Book* by Neil Gaiman, adapted by LAMDA from *The Graveyard Book*, 2008, Bloomsbury Publishing PLC **Gordon, Mick** *The Ride Of Your Life* Used by permission of Oberon Books **Gow, Michael** *All Stops Out* by Michael Gow. Copyright © 1991. First published by Currency Press 1991. Reproduced by permission from Currency Press Pty Ltd, Sydney, Australia www.currency.com.au **Gray, Keith** Adapted from *Ostrich Boys* by Keith Gray. Published by Definitions. Reprinted by permission of The

Random House Group Ltd (World excluding US and dependencies); copyright © 2008 by Keith Gray. Used by permission of Random House Children's Books, a division of Random House, Inc. Any third party use of this material, outside of this publication, is prohibited. Interested parties must apply directly to Random House for permission (US and Canada) **Grenfell-Hill, Jeffrey** *All I Want Is Scruffy Back*, *The Fossil Hunters*, *In Portia's Kitchen* and *Waiting* Used by permission of Jeffrey Grenfell-Hill **Griffith, Pansy** *Errol and the Ghost* Adapted by LAMDA. Used by permission of Pansy Griffith **Gupta, Tanika** *Fragile Land* © Tanika Gupta, 2003. Reprinted with permission of Oberon Books **Inglis, Andrea** *Robots-R-Us Dot Com* Used by permission of Andrea Inglis **Jamieson, Phil** *Believe It Or Not* and *There's Nothing To It* Used by permission of Phil Jamieson **Jones, Diana Wynne** Extracts adapted for dramatisation from *Howl's Moving Castle* © Diana Wynne Jones, 1986 (HarperCollins Children's Books) and *The Merlin Conspiracy* © Diana Wynne Jones, 2003 (HarperCollins Children's Books). Permission granted by the Estate of Diana Wynne Jones **Jury, Clifford** *Acting Class*, *In Control* and *Penalty*! Used by permission of Clifford Jury **Kehret, Peg** *The Stepsister Speaks Out* Used by permission of Meriwether Publishing **Kinsella, Sophie** *Confessions of a Shopaholic* Adapted from *Confessions of a Shopaholic* by Sophie Kinsella. Published by Black Swan. Reprinted by permission of The Random House Group Limited and Lucas Alexander Whitley **Korman, Gordon** *Son of Interflux* Adapted by LAMDA. Copyright © 1986 by Gordon Korman. First appeared in *Son of Interflux*, published by Scholastic. Reprinted by permission of Curtis Brown Ltd **Kosaki, Christina** *Evil Cat* Used by permission of Christina Kosaki **Larson, D M** *Teen Angel* and *Unicorns and Alley Cats* Used by permission of D M Larson (www.freedrama.net) **Lindgren, Astrid** *The Brothers Lionheart* Translated by Joan Tate and adapted by LAMDA. Used by permission of Saltkråkan **McCullough, L E** *Squeak and Maiow!* Used by permission of Smith and Kraus Publishers **McKenna, Shaun** *Below Stairs* and *The Player* Used by permission of Shaun McKenna **McLeod, Eleanor** *Snow White and the Seven Dwarfs* Used by permission of Eleanor McLeod. From *Scenes for Young Performers to Enjoy (Volume 1 Monologues)* published by Checkpoint Press 9781906628413 **Mauro, Robert** *Slob School* from *On Stage!* by Robert Mauro. Copyright 1990 Meriwether Publishing Ltd. Used by permission. www.meriwether.com **Mitchell, Adrian** *The Wild Animal Song Contest* Reprinted by permission of United Agents on behalf of The Estate of the late Julian Mitchell **Morpurgo, Clare and Michael** *Where My Wellies Take Me* Published by Templar Publishing and adapted by LAMDA. Used by permission of David Higham Associates **Odden, Anne** *The Date* Used by permission of Anne Odden **O'Hare, Jill** *The Necklace of Fingers* By permission of Dramatic Lines **Pearson, Kit** From *The Daring Game* by Kit Pearson, adapted by LAMDA. Copyright © Kathleen Pearson 1987. Reprinted by permission of Penguin Canada Books Inc **Pickering, Kenneth** *Come On* and *You Can't Do That!* Used by permission of Dramatic Lines Publishers **Powell, Kellie** *Dogface* Used by permission of the author (www.notmyshoes.net) **Pratchett, Terry** Extract from *The Amazing Maurice and his Educated Rodents* Terry Pratchett, adapted by Adrian Flynn (Oxford Playscripts, OUP, 2003), copyright © Stephen Briggs 2003, reprinted by permission of Oxford University Press **Price, Clare** *Apple Scramble*, *The Final Snore* and *A Maple Leaf Wonder* Used by permission of the author and Apple Pie Publications **Roddy, Ruth Mae** *Molly* Used by permission of Dramaline Publications **Shaw, George Bernard** *Androcles and the Lion* Used by permission of The Society of Authors, on behalf of the Bernard Shaw Estate **Smith, Dodie** *The Hundred and One Dalmatians* adapted by LAMDA. Used by permission of Film Rights Ltd in association with Laurence Fitch Ltd **Stephens, Heather** *Never the Bridesmaid* Used by permission of Dramatic Lines **Stoker, Jacqueline** *Under Hypnosis* Used by permission of Jacqueline Stoker **Stover, Joseph McNair** *The Mirror* Used by permission of Dramatic Lines Publishers **Swale, Jessica** *Blue Stockings* Used by permission of Jessica Swale and Macnaughton Lord **Teed, Nick** *Never Could Say Goodbye*, *Vicious Circle* and *Victims* Used by permission of Nick Teed **Thornton, Jenny** *Evacuee* and *Time* Used by permission of Jenny Thornton **Tinniswood, Emma-Louise** *Good Impressions* Used by permission of Emma-Louise Tinniswood **Wilson, Jacqueline** *Best Friends* Adapted by David Lawson Lean. From *Best Friends* by Jacqueline Wilson, published by Random House Children's Books. Used by permission of David Higham Associates **Wyndham, John** Adapted by LAMDA from *The Midwich Cuckoos* by John Wyndham (Penguin). Used by permission of David Higham Associates.